Sacred Mushroom/Holy Grail

TERRY ATKINSON

SACRED MUSHROOM/HOLY GRAIL

The Long-lost Origin of Our Most Intriguing Legend

ISBN-10: 0988412241
ISBN-13: 978-0-9884122-4-8

Library of Congress Control Number: 2013952618

Cover and formatting: Keith Carlson

First edition

Jorvik Press
PMB 424, 5331 SW Macadam Ave., Ste 258,
Portland OR 97239
JorvikPress.com

ABOUT THE AUTHOR

Terry Atkinson has had a long career as a journalist, columnist and editor. For the *Los Angeles Times* he created and edited the Home Tech section and wrote several columns including "L.A. Beat" and "Sound and Vision." For the L.A. Times Syndicate he wrote the weekly feature "Sound Advice." His work has also appeared in such publications as *Rolling Stone* and *American Film*. Atkinson's wide range of interests led to the discoveries revealed in *Sacred Mushroom/Holy Grail: The Long-lost Origin of Our Most Intriguing Legend*. He lives in Portland, Oregon.

CONTENTS

PREFACE

"So forget any ideas you got about lost cities, exotic travel, and digging up the world. We do not follow maps to buried treasure, and X never, ever marks the spot. Seventy percent of all archaeology is done in the library – research, reading."

Harrison Ford as Indiana Jones in
Indiana Jones and the Last Crusade

Good advice. However, it isn't long into the third of Steven Spielberg's Indiana Jones thrillers before its professor-archeologist-adventurer hero contradicts his own stay-on-campus advice. He's soon off in search of a supposedly very real lost treasure – nothing less than the ultimate lost treasure, the Holy Grail.

Last Crusade is very much in the tradition of all those motion pictures, books and other fictions about quests for the Grail that involve an allegedly actual artifact, usually the chalice from which Jesus Christ drank at the Last Supper. So no one should be shocked when Spielberg and associates (including mythmaker George Lucas, who co-wrote the story) fell right in line with most previous tellers of the Grail legend lock, stock and barrel – or at least lost treasure, stock clichés, and same old Christ cup.

This popular tradition is a long one. It basically dates back to the 15th Century's Thomas Malory, who gathered various characters and episodes from earlier Grail tales to concoct his *Le Morte D'Arthur*, and extends through Hollywood movies like *Last Crusade* and *Excalibur*. It makes for a good story. But not good scholarship.

The same goes for Dan Brown's *The Da Vinci Code*, the latest popular adventure woven around the Grail. Brown's novel, the greatest publishing phenomenon of the 21st Century so far (over 80 million copies sold as of 2009; translated into 44 languages) has excited readers by straying from the Grail-as-chalice concept, adapting the Grail-as-Christ's-bloodline approach taken from Michael Baigent, Richard Leigh and Henry Lincoln's earlier work,

Holy Blood, Holy Grail. However, that approach is pure balderdash based on a hoax, as clearly shown in rebuttals such as Martin Lunn's *The Da Vinci Code Decoded* and Carl Olson's and Sandra Miesel's *The Da Vinci Hoax*. For briefer examinations of Brown's nonsense, see Laura Miller's *New York Times Book Review* article, "The Da Vinci Con," or the excellent summary of objections, "Criticisms of *The Da Vinci Code*," that can be found at wikipedia.com, the Internet encyclopedia.

So what about good scholarship regarding the Grail legend? It didn't occur much until a boom in Arthurian studies began in the late 19th Century. Ever since then, one scholar after another has determined that the Grail was *not* Christ's chalice or anything like it. Originally, they've made clear, it was a mythological symbol representing something from the deep, dark past, something too sacred and/or secret to be identified.

That, of course, has not deterred seekers of the Grail. Instead of hunting for a tangible lost treasure, however, most now search for the spiritual meaning of the symbol – and for a way to incorporate its metaphysical dimensions into their lives. In accordance with these modern questers' needs, there has been a flood of hopefully inspirational New Age books interpreting the legend in those terms.

Actually, as it turns out, the Grail is more real than most recent explicators and fabricators imagine, but in a very different way from that assumed by the old-school searchers. And the way to this real Grail – that is, to finding the reality mysteriously conveyed by the earliest-known medieval stories about the icon – lies just where Professor Jones, rather than adventurer Indiana, said it was: in research, reading.

The volume you are reading is the result of such book-bound endeavors, and it offers a new theory about the true source of the Grail legend.

That source, I intend to show, was a toadstool.

Did a real food serve as the basis for Greek mythology's food of the gods, Ambrosia? In the 1950s a world-famous poet, novelist and historian determined that one did indeed – and he suggested what that food was.

Could anyone ever come up with a widely accepted explanation for the long-sought-after identity of the Hindu god/plant Soma? In the 1960s, someone did – a Wall Street banker, of all people. The solution was the same edible substance that the poet had associated with Ambrosia.

And in 1970 Doubleday published a book proposing a new theory about the origins of Christianity, written by the philologist who had been the British representative on the original team of scholars assigned to investigate the Dead Sea Scrolls. The secret encrypted into the gospels, he argued, was, once again, the wonder of nature that the other two scholars had revealed as an integral, if hidden, part of the Hindu religion and Greek mythology.

The poet-novelist-historian was Robert Graves, renowned for his studies, *The Greek Myths* and *The White Goddess*, his novel, *I, Claudius,* and his many volumes of poetry. He proposed in more than one essay that *Amanita muscaria*, the red-and-white-topped mushroom frequently used for illustrations in children's books, had been the Greek Food of the Gods.

The banker was former J.P. Morgan vice president R. Gordon Wasson, who argued in his book *Soma: Divine Mushroom of Immortality* that the same hallucinatory fungus, also known as fly agaric, had been the source for the *Rig-Veda*'s Soma.

And the linguist was University of Manchester professor John M. Allegro, part of the original team that studied the Dead Sea Scrolls, who proclaimed in his book *The Sacred Mushroom and the Cross* that the New Testament was a coded text referring throughout to *Amanita muscaria.*

These would not be the only works inspired by AM (as *Amanita muscaria* will be abbreviated herein). Literary scholars have noted that Lewis Carroll read a magazine article on the mushroom's effects shortly before relating the adventures of *Alice in Wonderland*. Decades later reclusive novelist Thomas Pynchon, in his most famous book, *Gravity's Rainbow,* wrote about a character who cultivated AM (even though no one has really learned how to produce this "toadstool," which grows in the wild in symbiosis with oak, birch, pine and certain other trees), boiled the brightly colored caps, dried the result and rolled it into cigarettes.

Another acclaimed novelist, Tom Robbins (*Even Cowgirls Get the Blues*), wrote a magazine article about AM titled "Superfly: The Mushroom That Conquered the Universe." And renowned playwright Paddy Chayefsky, author of such classic television plays as *Marty* and *Requiem for a Heavyweight*, composed the short novel *Altered States* (later made into a film starring William Hurt) about a scientist who undergoes a profound transformation after ingesting heavy doses of AM mixed with another vision-inducing plant.

The following book introduces a new theory regarding *Amanita muscaria*. It proposes that AM is the source of the legend of the Holy Grail. It also suggests new possibilities concerning AM, other aspects of Celtic mythology, and shamanism.

This is, in other words, one of those "crackpot" books. However, before being so sure that there are serious leaks in this cauldron of research, I ask the reader – like a knight entering the deep, dark, but promising forests of the Grail stories – to sally forth a while before coming to any conclusions.

PART ONE: THE MYSTERY AND THE EVIDENCE

THE GRAIL: MARVEL, METAPHOR, MYSTERY

The legends of the Grail have an enthralling atmosphere of mystery, of some tremendous secret which stays tantalizingly just outside the mind's grasp, in the shadows beyond the edge of conscious awareness. The outlines of the secret become clearer as writer after writer takes up the theme and makes his own sense of it, but we are never told in plain language exactly what the Grail means....

The heart of the myth is the idea of an object of awesome sanctity and power, which holds the secret of life. The stories, for all their diversity, are about a hero winning his way to this object, making himself master of it and penetrating its mystery.

Richard Cavendish, *King Arthur and the Grail*

Ever since it first appeared in written form more than 800 years ago, the legend of the Holy Grail has captured the interest of people in a uniquely powerful way. The Grail has become Western civilization's ultimate metaphor for something most dearly desired and pursued.

A baseball player's Holy Grail is winning the World Series. An investor's Holy Grail is buying a stock at 10, having it balloon to 200, and selling at exactly the right time. A gambler's Holy Grail is breaking the bank at Monte Carlo or putting a serious dent in the profits of a Las Vegas casino.

The Grail image permeates our language largely because the Grail legend has been told many times in many ways, enchanting and inspiring us with the story of a mystical object and a perilously difficult quest for it. To this day the Grail remains a vital theme in literature, opera, film and other arts, striking a resonant chord with the millions who have encountered its extraordinary nature.

However, this great symbol has been enveloped in great misunderstanding. The most popular versions of the legend differ radically from the earliest known story of the Grail, which was, in fact, called "The Story of the Grail," if we translate into English its Old French title, *Le Conte du Graal*.

This "Story" was the last tale written by Chrétien de Troyes, the greatest writer of medieval romances, the imaginative prose and verse narratives generally dealing with the adventures of young men (often knights) dedicated to the pursuit of romantic love or some other high ideal. In the middle and late 12th Century, Chrétien wrote a series of romances for the court of Marie de Champagne, daughter of Eleanor of Aquitaine, though he dedicated his final work to another French royal, Philip of Flanders.

Also known as *Perceval*, after the name of its protagonist, *Le Conte du Graal* was left unfinished by Chrétien at the time of his death around 1190. However, partly due to the popularity of his previous romances (such as *Erec et Enide, Cliges,* and *Yvain*), and partly due to the intriguing nature of this *graal* (as Chrétien spelled it), other authors completed *Le Conte du Graal* in what are known as the four "Continuations." These were soon followed by several other Grail romances which appeared not only in France but also in other parts of Europe.

Quite understandably, considering the church's influence in medieval Europe, almost all of these subsequent versions added strong Christian elements to the relatively few Chrétien had included. And, just as understandably, the subsequent Grail stories strengthened the connections to King Arthur's court that were tenuous in *Le Conte du Graal*. In addition, they substituted more conventionally heroic (or at least determined) knights for Chrétien's often stumbling, bumbling "hero," Perceval.

The Grail stories became a central part of what became known collectively as Arthurian literature, a body of work that, though initially popular in French and other continental courts, was derived from elsewhere – across the English Channel.

A CHANGING STORY

Le Conte du Graal, like most of Chrétien's romances, was based on a story that had been imported into Europe from the British Isles after the Norman Conquest of 1066. Most of these tales had their origin in the rich oral literary tradition of the Celts, who had once inhabited most of Britain but had been pushed by invading Germanic peoples to the west and north, primarily into Scotland, Wales and Ireland.

In his *The King and the Corpse: Tales of the Soul's Conquest of Evil,* the great mythologist Heinrich Zimmer explains the process that led to the Christian European adoption and corruption of Celtic and other northern European religious and literary traditions:

"The growth of the heathen religions of northern Europe was nipped in the bud when the peoples who had practiced them came within the sphere of Christian influence. The church did more than Roman culture to deprive the mythology of the Celts, the Teutons, and the pre-Celtic primitive population of the British Isles of the old creed in which it lived, moved, and had its being. Nevertheless it survived, without foundation or foothold, no longer a cult, and shorn of its ancient ritual. As elsewhere under similar circumstances, mythology became transformed into poetry and saga, became secularized, and lost its binding power; and since in this form there was nothing about it that the church could attack, it continued to develop through the Middle Ages, supplying a rich nourishment for the soul, when the church with its theology of salvation had nothing comparable to offer. Medieval man dreamed out his broken youth in the images and figures of Celtic and pre-Celtic myths and sagas; and it was these, in the form of the Grail and other romances of the Arthurian cycle, that became the popular novels of the knightly and courtly circles of the whole of Europe."

This craze for stories about King Arthur, his knights and the Holy Grail lasted only a few decades, diminishing after 1230. However, as Emma Jung (the wife of psychologist Carl Jung) and Marie-Louise von Franz noted in their *The Grail Legend*, "a mass of transcripts, translations and, at a later date, printings [appeared] which prove that the story did not cease to exercise its magic, spellbinding influence down through the centuries."

Strong, widespread interest was revived after William Caxton printed (and titled) in 1485 a literary work that Sir Thomas Malory had written fifteen years before while confined in Newgate Prison. *Le Morte D'Arthur* established the basis of most popular Arthurian and Grail fiction to follow.

"That a book of such nobility should have been written by a violent criminal," Richard Cavendish notes in his lucid study, *King Arthur and the Grail*, "surprises even those who do not share the common delusion that a great artist must also be a good man."

Until Malory, Grail (indeed, all Arthurian) literature had been a hodgepodge of roughly related and often conflicting narratives. By choosing elements from those early manuscripts (mainly what's called "The Vulgate Cycle," a series of five anonymous manuscripts written in French prose between 1215 and 1230) and bolstering the

Christian-quest theme, Malory laid the foundation for most renditions to follow. Among these: Alfred Lord Tennyson's poetic and extremely influential interpretation, *Idylls of the King*, T.H. White's fantasy *The Once and Future King*, Richard Wagner's opera *Parsifal*, novels like John Cowper Powys's *A Glastonbury Romance* and Richard Monarco's *Parsifal, The Grail War* and *The Final Quest*, and such motion pictures as *The Silver Chalice, Parsifal* (there have been at least three films with this title) and *Excalibur*.

It is from this post-Malory tradition that our modern concept of the Grail has been derived – how it was supposedly the chalice from Christ's Last Supper, found and brought to the British Isles by Joseph of Arimathea, there buried or somehow lost, then sought after by King Arthur's knights. Other repeated themes include the Grail's hovering appearance at Arthur's Round Table, its containing the sacred blood of Christ, its final achievement by the knight who possessed the purest heart, and his ascension to heaven with it.

However, none of these elements are in the first Grail story.

THE MANY FORMS OF THE GRAIL

"People who mention the Holy Grail generally think of it as a holy relic, the cup used by Christ at the Last Supper," wrote the British historian Geoffrey Ashe in his renowned study, *King Arthur's Avalon: The Story of Glastonbury*. "They generally have the notion that an antique legend describes Joseph of Arimathea as bringing it to Britain. After its arrival it was buried or otherwise lost at Glastonbury.

"Those who take this conventional view are wrong on all counts. The Grail makes its entry, not as a relic, but as a talisman. Its Christian guise is an afterthought... No genuine popular or monastic tradition has a word to say about it in the religious aspect, and its connection to Glastonbury, though indissoluble, is enigmatic."

In Chrétien's "Story," the object in question is not even identified as a cup. And it is called a *graal* – lower case, no capitalization, no "the" signifying that it's the only one of its kind. A *graal* was, to quote the early 13th-century writer Hélinand of Froidmont, "a wide and somewhat deep dish in which expensive meats are customarily placed for the rich."

However, the *graal* Perceval witnesses in the castle of the Fisher King, as described in more detail in the next chapter, is no ordinary platter. It is made of pure gold and inlaid with precious gems "of many kinds, the richest and the costliest that exist in the sea or in the earth." Though Chrétien describes this *graal* no further, he notes that the woman who carries it is "beautiful, gracious, splendidly garbed," and when she enters there is "such a brilliant light that the candles lost their brightness, just as the stars do when the moon or the sun rises."

In subsequent romances, the Grail takes many forms - including platter, chalice, and gemstone - and it is associated with other objects, primarily lances and swords. Sometimes it is identified as a ciborium, a vessel containing a sacred host or remnant, generally with an arched cover surmounted by a cross.

The description of the Grail that differs most radically from the later-accepted concept is the one found in Wolfram von Eschenbach's *Parzival*. This Bavarian work, written sometime between 1200 and 1212, is considered by most modern scholars to have the highest literary quality of the early Grail stories, and it served as the basis for Richard Wagner's final opera *Parsifal*. Yet Wolfram's Grail, "which surpasses all earthly perfection," is a "stone," probably a rare gem, possibly a large emerald.

The confusion regarding the original romances doesn't end there. Chrétien's central protagonist is a would-be knight who is more fool than hero, and whose actions are often far from commendable. In subsequent versions the protagonists' names, aims and personalities varied greatly, as did the nature of their adventures.

This disorder largely stems from the fact that Chrétien left *Le Conte du Graal* unfinished. The Continuations and other renditions that followed included Robert de Boron's *Perceval*, the so-called Vulgate Cycle (including the *Queste del Saint Graal*) and the also-anonymous *Perlesvaus*.

THE BASIC STORY

Though the many Grail stories and continuations of 1180-1230 vary greatly and even sometimes conflict with each other, most of the early and important romances share essential elements and tell the same basic tale.

A young man, generally a knight (who is sometimes part of a contingent of King Arthur's knights), who has embarked on a quest – either specifically for the Grail or for a vaguer spiritual or self-discovery goal – comes upon a deep forest or a wasteland in which lies an eerie castle that is the home of a maimed Fisher King (as well as, in some versions, a more mysterious second king).

There the visitor beholds a lance with blood dripping from its tip or a sword said to have magical properties, or both. He is treated to a feast throughout which parades a strange procession of servants and objects, including a maiden or maidens carrying in the brilliantly glowing, jewel-encrusted and often golden (but otherwise obscurely described) Grail. Despite all the odd events, the young man holds his tongue and asks no questions. Later, he is told by a strange woman or a holy hermit that this reticence was a grave mistake. By failing to ask any question – particularly a key one, which he's later told in some versions is "Whom does the Grail serve?" – he has missed his opportunity to heal the Fisher King, and, by magical association, the travails of his kingdom.

THE QUEST FOR MEANING

The Grail legend sparked a great deal of scholarly interest. Particularly since the latter part of the 19th Century there have been many efforts to collect, date, interpret and investigate the manuscripts of the late 12th and early 13th Centuries.

The goal of many scholars, of course, has been to locate the wellspring from which the legend emerged. As Richard Cavendish wrote in his essay on the Grail in *Man, Myth and Magic*: "The origins of the Grail have been searched for in Christianity, in paganism, in Byzantine, Persian, Jewish and Mohammedan traditions. Traces of Gnostic ideas have been revealed, and hints of possible Templar and Cathar influences. For the different stories that have come down to us vary very considerably, and the great American authority R.S. Loomis plaintively observed that 'the authors of the Grail texts seem to delight in contradicting each other on the most important points.'

"The stories contradict each other," Cavendish explained, "because there is no single Grail legend but a number of variants embroidering on not one but several themes. They tend to be rambling and inconsistent because they were originally told, not written."

The quest for the legend's beginning point has been almost as confused as those contradictory original texts themselves. However, there are a couple of points almost all scholars have agreed upon – 1. The Christian elements were tacked on to a tale of pagan origin, and 2. The first Western European authors of Grail narratives drew the basic elements of their tales from the Celtic oral tradition of the British Isles.

Actually, as we shall see, the Grail legend has even more ancient roots. However, Celtic mythology does indeed hold the freshest and most valuable clues. The legend's Celtic background not only strongly suggests that something real gave rise to the legend, but also provides revelatory indications of what that reality was.

We shall begin our search for the solution to the Grail mystery by following this "line of inquiry" – Celtic mythology. Eventually, this path will lead us to another rich field of clues, shamanism. First, though, I'll present a synopsis of the very first Grail story, Chrétien des Troyes' *Le Conte du Graal.* Most of my conjectures will be based upon the material found in this work, partly because it is the earliest known version of the legend and partly because many (if not all) of the subsequent tellings depend on it to one extent or another.

As Jean Markale wrote in *The Grail: The Celtic Origins of the Sacred Icon*: "From the chronological perspective, which forms a solid system of reference, Chrétien de Troyes seems to be the initiator of the Grail legend. One can get a clear idea of Chrétien's primary importance through simple consideration of the widespread and enormous fortune his legend has enjoyed. In the end, from the literary standpoint not a single work dealing with the subject of the Grail can be considered as independent – either wholly or partly – from [it]."

The chapter summarizing Chrétien's "Story of the Grail" will be followed by a brief overview of the more significant other early European manuscripts dealing with the legend. However, both of these chapters are optional – the reader may chose to skip them without missing a whole lot, because when we reach the part dealing with the solution to the mystery of the Grail legend, we will be referring back to the most revealing clues in these often confusing (and confused) adventures.

THE STORY OF THE GRAIL

Compared to the Grail stories appearing in works by Malory or Tennyson, or in innumerable retellings aimed at adults and (most often) children, Chrétien de Troyes' *Le Conte du Graal* is a rather wild and woolly tale.

Prepare yourself. Chrétien, like other writers of these earliest Grail tales, was working from Celtic sources that he only partially understood. On top of that, he wove in elements that would make these exotic stories palatable to their readers or patrons. As a result, consistency and narrative sense are hardly the outstanding qualities of these epics.

The patron in Chrétien's case was Philip of Flanders, who actually – Chrétien's introduction tells us – found the source book himself. What resulted, though unfinished, contains many of the key elements of (and therefore clues to) the Grail tradition – including the brave fool Perceval, the Fisher King, Arthur and his knights (with emphasis on Gawain), and, of course, the Grail (*graal*) itself, making its first appearance in written-down Western literature.

AN UNCOUTH YOUTH

The tale begins deep in a Welsh forest. Perceval has been raised there by his mother, who hopes to guard him from the ways of the world. However, when her son is a young man, he comes upon five knights. Their glittering armor leads him to first believe that they are angels. But when he learns that they are from the court of King Arthur, he questions his mother about them. She tells him what she has hidden from him until then: that his father had been a knight, too, one who was physically maimed by a wound in the thigh and died from grief when he learned that his other two sons had been killed. The mother had fled into the woods to protect Perceval from a similar fate.

Perceval becomes dead set on going to King Arthur to become a knight himself. His mother dresses him in a ridiculous-looking rustic outfit, hoping he will be laughed out of court.

Perceval seems unlikely knightly material. He is ignorant of such things as religion, chivalry or even the most basic civilized manners – though his mother gives him some hasty teaching about Christ and the Church and how to behave honorably toward women just before he leaves. He doesn't even seem to be a very good son – when he parts from his mother she faints, but he simply spurs on his horse. And the first thing he does after setting off is to assault a young woman!

He comes upon a tent, finds a lady sleeping inside, forces a kiss upon her, and steals her ring.

Later, directed by a peasant, Perceval finds Arthur's castle at Carlisle. Nearing it, he passes a knight dressed in red armor, who is carrying a golden goblet stolen from the king's table. The Red Knight orders Perceval to take a challenge to Arthur.

Perceval rides straight into the great hall of Arthur's castle, butting his horse against the king, who graciously overlooks this breach in etiquette and lets Perceval know what a bad sort this Red Knight is: the bounder has not only stolen the cup but spilled its contents all over the queen.

Perceval declares that if Arthur will make him a knight he'll take care of the crimson-colored culprit. Has our boy suddenly taken on the sort of noble character we associate with Arthur's knights? Well, not entirely. He covets the Red Knight's armor to cover the ridiculously rustic clothing mom dressed him in.

Speaking of ridicule, it's immediately heaped on Perceval by Arthur's seneschal. The Queen's handmaiden speaks up for Perceval, stating her belief that the young intruder will eventually prove himself the best knight in the world. The seneschal strikes her down.

Does Perceval come to her aid? No. Instead, he rides off after the Red Knight, not even waiting for Arthur to reply to the request for knighthood. He's followed by one of the king's squires.

Our young hero – or is it anti-hero? – catches up with the Red Knight and kills him by hurling a javelin through the man's eye. The squire helps him strip off the red armor. He gives his horse and the stolen cup to the squire, ordering him to tell that damned seneschal that he'll pay for striking the handmaiden.

By now the reader should be expecting odd behavior from Perceval, and once again he doesn't let us down. Instead of heading for Arthur's court himself, he heads into the forest for some unspecified reason – now dressed in the Red Knight's armor and riding the departed ruffian's horse.

Coming upon a river he cannot cross, Perceval follows the bank until he comes upon another castle. The lord there, Gornemont, keenly recognizes that this stranger is "uncouth and silly of speech," and after hearing of his adventure offers help.

He gives Perceval a lesson in arms and horsemanship, and tells him that if he's going to be a knight he'd better learn to aid damsels in distress, have mercy on defeated opponents, to become a good Christian, and "beware also of talking too much and of gossiping." Perceval says that his mother also warned him about asking too many questions.

Unfortunately, this last advice will cause Perceval to commit a crucial error in the soon-to-follow central episode of the tale.

THE GRAIL CASTLE

Perceval sets off again, and we finally learn what he's about: he's trying to find his way back to mom. After riding back into the forest he's soon distracted from returning home but he gets to show off his would-be knightly skills by freeing a young woman who is besieged there from an evil knight.

Eventually, while following the bank of a river, he spots a boat with two men in it. One of them is baiting a hook. Perceval asks them if there is any place to ford the stream. The fisherman answers that there is no such place nearby but offers him lodging in "the house where I dwell, near the river and near the wood." Perceval follows the man's directions, ascending the bank but seeing no house where it was said to be. He believes that he's been deceived.

But there suddenly appears a structure – not a mere house but a magnificent castle with three towers, a great hall and an arcade. Four squires remove Perceval's armor and drape him in "a scarlet mantle, fresh and new." He is led to a square hall.

Now begins the central and most mysterious episode of the story.

In the hall, on a couch before the fire, sits "a handsome nobleman." He rises with difficulty to greet his guest. (Perceval doesn't realize it, but he'll later learn that this is the same man who was fishing the river.) As Perceval talks with this lord, a squire enters carrying a sword.

This sword has been so finely forged that it is practically unbreakable, says the nobleman, who, to Perceval's surprise, presents it to him, saying the weapon was destined to be his.

Something stranger still happens next.

Another squire enters, holding a white lance by its middle. He passes between the fire and the two men. From the point of this lance "a drop of red blood ran down to the squire's hand."

Perceval would like to ask what this means, but he remembers the advice against too much speech, and he's afraid of being rude.

Then two more squires come in, "bearing in their hands candelabra of fine gold and niello work [deep-black metal-alloy inlay]." In each candelabrum were "at least ten lighted candles."

A damsel follows the squires, holding between her hands a grail (*un graal*). Chrétien tells us that this object is of pure gold and richly set with precious gems "of many kinds, the richest and the costliest that exist in the sea or in the earth," but he does not describe it further. The woman is "beautiful, gracious, splendidly garbed," and when she enters there is "such a brilliant light that the candles lost their brightness, just as the stars do when the moon or the sun rises."

She is followed by another maiden holding "a carving platter of silver." Both women, like the squires before them, pass between the two men and the fire. Still, Perceval does not dare to say anything.

The master of the castle then calls for washing water and the table prepared for the meal. A broad ivory table is set up on two ebony supports in front of the couch. It is covered with a snow-white cloth.

As the men enjoy their first course, the Grail is carried before them again. With every dish the same thing occurs, the Grail appearing "*trestot decouvert*" (quite uncovered). But no matter how much Perceval marvels at this strange ceremony, he cannot bring himself to ask questions about it.

He decides that he'll inquire the next day. But when morning comes, he is alone. No one answers his knocking and calling. He finds his horse saddled and the drawbridge lowered. With a leap he just makes it across as the drawbridge rises behind him. He calls out one last time, and finally rides off unanswered.

Very soon after, Perceval finds out that he has erred in not asking about the dream-like events of the night before.

EDUCATION AND QUEST

Riding away from the castle, he comes upon a maiden weeping over the body of her lover, a knight who has been decapitated. After Perceval and the young woman discuss what happened to the knight, she asks where he's come from. When he tells her, she asks "Did you lie then at the dwelling of the rich Fisher King?"

"I do not know if he is fisherman or king," Perceval replies, "but he is very rich and courteous." The maiden assures him that his host is a king, one who had been maimed in battle. "A javelin wounded him through the two thighs." The wound will not heal and he can no longer mount a horse, but diverts himself with fishing. "Therefore, he is called the Fisher King."

Then the maiden asks him about each of the apparitions before and during the meal, and whether he inquired about their meaning. When Perceval says no, she cries: "So help me God, learn, then, that you have done ill." She says that instead of Perceval of Wales he should be called Perceval the Wretched, because if he had asked about these things - and the Grail in particular - he would have cured the Fisher King and great good would have resulted.

The maiden attributes his failure to his "sin" - the neglect of his mother, who, she further informs him, has died of sorrow. Now Perceval faces misery ahead. For one thing, the sword the Fisher King gave him will betray him at a crucial moment and break into pieces. Fortunately, the maiden also gave him the name of the only smith - one Trebuchet - able to repair it.

Perceval locates Arthur's court, but his welcome is interrupted by the appearance of a hideous woman. Before everyone, this Loathly Damsel berates Perceval for the way he behaved at the Grail castle. "Was it so irksome then to open your mouth and ask the reason why those drops of blood spilled from the white iron?" she asks. "And of the Grail you saw you equally did not inquire and did not ask what rich man was served therewith."

As a result of his inaction, she says, the lands about the Grail castle would be laid waste and people would suffer and die.

Turning back to Arthur, she asks if he has heard of the Chastel Orgueilleux (Castle of Pride), where knightly deeds are needed, or Montesclaire, where a maiden is besieged. Whoever frees this damsel will win the highest fame and *l'espee as estranges renges* (the sword with the strange baldric).

Perhaps the strangest thing about this is that Arthur's knights take her seriously and prepare to march off toward these challenges.

However, the shamed Perceval has other plans. He vows never to spend two nights in the same place and to endure all sufferings until he discovers why the lance bled and whom the Grail served.

ENTER GAWAIN

Now, Perceval may seem an odd story to you so far, and it takes perhaps its strangest turn at this point.

Chrétien temporarily turns the spotlight away from Perceval and places it on Gauvain (aka Gawain), one of Arthur's knights. We will consider this and other early Grail literature references to Gawain in an upcoming chapter.

However, let me note here before we get back to Perceval, that Gawain winds up, after various fights and adventures, on a quest for the very "bleeding lance" that Perceval witnessed in the Grail castle, though at the request of yet another ruler, the King of Escavalon.

We shall find that Jung and von Franz, as well as Weston, have some very interesting things to say about the parallel yet differing nature of these two knights' quests – one for the masculine lance, the other for the feminine platter, bowl or cup known as the Grail. But for now...

A HERMIT, A FISH, AND A LACK OF FINISH

When the story returns to Perceval, it is five years after the incident of the Loathly Damsel at Arthur's court. We are told that Perceval has had many adventures upon his quest to learn the meaning of what he observed at the Grail castle, but he has come no closer to an answer.

On Good Friday, he is berated (yes, again), this time by a procession of knights and ladies who are observing the holy day. They reprimand him for not doing so. Perceval, who has lost all remembrance of God and the church, follows them to a holy man's chapel where Mass is to be held. Giving confession to this hermit, Perceval tells him of his failure to aid the Fisher King.

When the hermit learns Perceval's name, he informs him that he is his uncle (his mother's brother) and that "he who is served from [the Grail] is my brother; the Rich Fisher is his son, and your mother was our sister."

And so Perceval learns not only that there are *two* kings in the Grail castle, but that he is related to both. The elder king is, like the hermit, a maternal uncle, and thus Perceval's cousin.

The hermit then immediately adds: "Do not imagine that perchance the Grail contains pike, lamprey or salmon," that is, a fish. "No, it is only by the Host [a single Mass-wafer] that is brought to him in this Grail that the holy man maintains life!"

Now this might seem the strangest yet of Perceval's many incongruities. However, as we shall eventually see in a later chapter, all this talk of fish is of great consequence in solving the mystery of the Grail legend.

The hermit adds that the Grail is so holy and the old king so spiritual that he has stayed alive for fifteen years on this diet of one Mass-wafer a day. He has never left his room in the castle during this time.

Perceval is granted absolution and advised to hear Mass every day. Then the hermit whispers in his ear a prayer that contains secret names of Christ, but this prayer must never be said "except in great peril."

After receiving Communion on Easter Day, Perceval rides off. We are not to read anything more about him in Chrétien's tale, because, after switching to some more of Gawain's adventures, *Le Conte du Graal* ends abruptly.

Despite their unfinished condition, manuscripts of Chrétien's last story became very popular soon after his death. So much so, in fact, that four "Continuations" of the story were concocted, as well as similar tales and other Grail-oriented literature. We shall consider these in the following chapter.

THE PLOT THICKENS: AN OVERVIEW OF OTHER EARLY GRAIL ROMANCES

The popularity of Chrétien's *Le Conte du Graal* opened a floodgate for Grail-oriented manuscripts over the following four decades. Markale has stated that "from the literary standpoint, not a single work dealing with the subject of the Grail can be considered as independent – either wholly or partly – from [Chrétien's version]." Whether that is so or not (and certainly many other Arthurian scholars are not sure), most of the Continuations and other subsequent versions strayed far from the earliest-known Grail story in almost every way. Even if they all drew inspiration from *Le Conte du Graal*, either directly or (in most cases) indirectly, their characters and events were largely derived from other sources – not the least of these being, of course, the authors' own imaginations.

Nevertheless, despite all their obviously (and sometimes not so obviously) added elements – ranging from the widespread attachment of Christian connections to wild flights of fancy – these later works sometimes indicate the use of pagan-based sources and offer their own intriguing clues. Since we will be dredging up those clues at the proper time, brief summaries of the more compelling manuscripts will do for now.

PEREDUR

Though it never mentions the Grail, the Welsh tale "Peredur" is almost always included in scholarly studies of the Grail legend because it so closely resembles Chrétien's story of the similar-sounding Perceval. Some writers have speculated that Peredur – found in two medieval manuscripts (*The Red Book of Hergest* and The *White Book of Rhydderch*) and collected in the 19th Century *Mabinogion* – was based directly on *Le Conte du Graal*. However, others believe that Chrétien's account and the tale told by the anonymous author(s) of *The Red Book* and *The White Book* were both based on the same Welsh traditional oral story, which they probably found translated in a French source manuscript that was since lost.

In Peredur we find, as with so many of the post-Chrétien texts, a mingling of the pagan, otherworldly Grail (or Grail-like) story with one of the standard types of Celtic literature (and most other literatures) – the revenge tale. This Welsh romance, first written down around 1200, bears an attribute that unfortunately marks most of the Grail romances – confusion. The confusion found in this and other narratives whose summaries follow makes Chrétien's abrupt switch from the adventures of Perceval to those of Gawain seem perfectly reasonable in comparison. Peredur, Loomis says, "is so very confused" that the author wove into his Celtic-based source material "memories of various French or Anglo-Norman romances."

In order to better understand how muddled these post-Chrétien tales become, let us – with patience we will not shower upon the rest – hack through some (though definitely not all) of Peredur's brambles, mainly focusing on those parts of the tale that bear a relationship to Chrétien's story of Perceval.

First, there's the hero's name, a Welsh one which, Loomis notes, "probably suggested to the French the name Perceval, 'Pierce-valley'...." Secondly, a long string of striking similarities to *Le Conte du Graal*. These begin with the way Peredur, like Perceval, is brought up by his mother away from society and the chivalrous pursuits that brought about the death of the boy's father and brothers. Peredur's emergence from this sheltered existence is spurred, as in Chrétien's tale, by the appearance of three of King Arthur's knights, one of whom is named Gwalchmai, a Welsh form of Gawain. The young man takes off for Arthur's court, where his rustic appearance and naive behavior is a source of amusement for those there.

Peredur sets off on his horse to prove himself, starting first with the finding and killing of an errant knight who has stolen Queen Guinevere's cup. After this and other adventures, he rides into "a vast and desert wood, on the confines of which was a lake." He spies on the other side of the lake a "fair castle," and on the shore of the body of water he sees "a venerable, hoary-headed man" whose "attendants were fishing in the lake." Upon spotting Peredur, the old man walks toward his palace, and our young hero, noticing that the elderly fellow is lame, follows him into the open door and enters a hall. There the Lame King (who turns out to be his maternal uncle) sits upon another cushion before a roaring fire. His servants greet and disarray Peredur, who is invited to sit beside the king and enjoy a meal with him.

The lameness of this king certainly reminds us of the maimed king of *Le Conte du Graal*, and there will be further correlations, but when

Peredur is given a sword at the end of the meal, he – unlike Perceval – is told to put it to immediate use.

After they finish their food, the king asks Peredur if he knows how to fight with a sword. The young man replies no, but he wouldn't mind being taught. The king introduces his two sons and tells Peredur to take the sword and fight one of them and "draw blood." Peredur does so, tearing open a gash in the youth's forehead. The king is pleased and informs Peredur that he is "thy mother's brother." Apparently having fonder feelings for his nephews than his sons, the king tells Peredur he will house and instruct him, and "raise thee to the rank of knight from this time forward."

Soon come the "obvious distortions, errors and inconsistencies" that cause Loomis to declare Peredur a "singularly incoherent narrative."

The next day, "with his uncle's permission," Peredur rides through the forest and comes upon another castle, where he passes through the open gate and beholds in the hall yet another "hoary-headed king," who, just like the first, hosts him to a fine feast and then asks him the same question: Can he fight with a sword?

"Were I to receive instruction," said Peredur, "I think I could."

The king gives Peredur a sword, but, many readers will be relieved to know, tells him to strike not some poor unfortunate relative but a huge, iron column. Our hero does so, somehow slicing the column in two – but also breaking the sword into the same number of pieces. He's told to put the sword back together and is magically able to. He repeats the cutting of the column and the reuniting of the sword pieces once more, but his third try is unsuccessful. This signifies, the king explains, that "thou hast arrived at two-thirds of thy strength... When thou attainest thy full power, none will be able to contend with thee."

Then *this* king announces that *he* is Peredur's maternal uncle! The author, Loomis groans, forgets that he has already had one king take that role.

Soon things get more interesting – or at least a lot bloodier.

Two youths enter the hall bearing "a spear of mighty size, with three streams of blood flowing from the point to the ground – certainly reminiscent of the spear Perceval witnessed. Though people about them lament and wail at the sight, the king takes little notice, and forbids Peredur to ask about the spear – not the same thing as Perceval's reluctance to ask questions, but certainly suggestive of it.

Next enter two maidens. Neither holds a luminous *graal*. But they do have something with them that Cavendish calls "an extraordinary metamorphosis of the Grail." The women carry "a large salver" (a serving tray) between them, and on it, lying in a pool of blood, is a man's head. Again, the company cries out. After they've quieted down, Peredur is allowed to retreat to a chamber to sleep and to leave the next day.

As he rides, he comes upon a beautiful woman beside a corpse. She, like the one who Perceval encounters, tells him that he has messed up. "When thou wast in the palace of the Lame King, and didst see there the youth bearing the streaming spear, from the point of which were drops of blood flowing in streams down to the hand of the youth, and many other wonders likewise, thou didst not inquire their meaning nor their cause. Hadst thou done so, the King would have been restored to health, and his dominions to peace." The king, as a result, would suffer a series of calamities, "and all this is because of thee."

Peredur replies that he "will not sleep tranquilly until I know the story and the meaning of the lance." He then undergoes what Loomis describes as "a series of irrelevant encounters with monsters, a battle, an abortive love affair, and other adventures..." Except for coming upon, near King Arthur's court, the Loathly Damsel, his journeys stray far from those of Chrétien's Perceval, including a fourteen-year period spent ruling alongside "the empress of great Constantinople."

Finally, he arrives at a castle in a valley, enters the hall, and is greeted by "a lame grey-headed man" besides which sits Gwalchmai. A youth kneels before the three and explains to Peredur the head on the salver was "thy cousin's, and he was killed by the sorceresses of Gloucester, who also lamed thine uncle; and I am thy cousin. There is a prediction that thou art to avenge these things." With the help of some of King Arthur's men, he accomplishes this vengeance, and the entangled tale ends.

"Independent references show that Peredur was a figure well established in Welsh tradition," writes University of Wales professor Brynley F. Roberts in *The Arthurian Encyclopedia*, "and it is possible that Peredur is a retelling in Welsh of material found in, or used by, Chrétien, combined with independent folklore and dynastic traditions about the hero. The Grail and its attendant mysteries are represented in Welsh by the head, and the tale becomes one of vengeance for the slaying of a kinsman."

As noted earlier, it has never been determined whether Peredur preceded or followed *Le Conte du Graal*. However, the manuscripts we'll deal with next definitely followed Chrétien's romance, simply because they are attempts to complete his unfinished story.

THE FOUR 'CONTINUATIONS' OF *LE CONTE DU GRAAL*

It is ironic that the earliest and most essential Grail tale, Chrétien's, is the only one that was left unfinished. Even more paradoxically, the very fact that *Le Conte du Graal* was incomplete probably accounted for a good deal of its popularity and for the popularity of the Grail legend as a whole. As John L. Grigsby wrote in an article in *The Arthurian Encyclopedia*, "Even Chrétien's failure became a momentous literary event, for his unfinished Perceval engendered writing and debate that have endured to the present. The mystery of the Grail, the Bleeding Lance, and the respective roles of Perceval and Gauvain were heady matters in the early thirteenth century..."

Early among the works inspired by this interest were several attempts to complete Chrétien's story, known as the "Continuations." As Grigsby notes, *Le Conte du Graal* "ends abruptly at line 9234 (in the Hilka text). A first continuator picked up the story at this point and added 9,500 to 19,600 lines (depending on the various manuscript traditions) but came to no conclusion. Since this First Continuation was once attributed to a Wauchier de Denain and then this attribution was disproved, this version became known as the Pseudo-Wauchier. A Second Continuation, which may have been written by a Gauchier de Donaing, added 13,000 more lines to the First but was still inconclusive. A third continuator, Manessier, added 10,000 lines and provides an ending, with Perceval crowned as Grail King. Gerbert de Montreuil wrote a Fourth Continuation of 17,000 lines and, ignoring Manessier, provided his own finish, where Perceval returns to the Grail Castle and mends the broken sword."

Altogether, then, the Continuations added more than 50,000 lines to the legend. There are some intriguing elements amid this annex, but the Grail tales of Robert de Boron offer more valuable clues.

ROBERT DE BORON'S TRILOGY

More significant than the Continuations, in terms of determining the Grail legend's roots, is the trilogy of romances composed by a Burgundian poet named Robert de Boron (aka Borron and Bouron). This is because the three parts of the trilogy – *Joseph D'Arimathe*, *Merlin* and *Perceval* – contain fascinating episodes that do not seem to be pure fancy.

De Boron's work is now thought to have come very close on the heels of Chrétien's writings. *Joseph* has been given a probable date of 1191-1202, though it was most likely written closer to the latter date, the year the patron for whom it was composed, Gautier de Montbéliard, departed for the Fourth Crusade. This first part of the cycle is also the only section that still exists in the original Old French octosyllabic verse. Most of *Merlin* (of which only 504 lines of the original exist) and all of *Perceval* are known to us through an anonymous prose adaptation made early in the 13th Century.

De Boron paradoxically provided both the chief feature of the Grail legend that Christianized it *and* the most telling post-Chrétien clue regarding the legend's secret pagan origin.

For the first time in Arthurian literature, *Joseph D'Arimathe* (aka *Romanz De L'estoire Dou Graal*) presents the Grail as Christ's chalice. De Boron apparently invented the story of how Joseph of Arimathea, the disciple of Jesus who provided the cave/tomb where the crucified Christ's body was laid, gained possession of the cup used at the Last Supper, collected some of Christ's blood in it, and transported the vessel to Britain.

However, this same story contains the obviously pagan-related section that has most intrigued Arthurian scholars. It involves Joseph's brother-in-law, Bron (who becomes known as the Rich Fisher, a variation of the Fisher King), the Grail, and a peculiar fish. As we shall see in a later chapter, this part of the tale is a key piece in solving the puzzle of the legend's true beginnings.

Robert's *Merlin* draws heavily on Geoffrey of Monmouth's description of the wizard. Merlin uses his magic to aid two sons of

Britain's King Constant, Pendragon and Uther, and, later, the son of the latter, Arthur. He also constructs the Round Table, which is modeled after the Grail Table at which Joseph held rituals with the cup of the Last Supper in the Holy Land.

In Robert's *Perceval* (aka the Didot-*Perceval*), Merlin, before retiring to the woods, helps Perceval become the Grail King and fill the seat of the Siege Perilous at Arthur's court.

THE DIDOT-*PERCEVAL* AND *PERLESVAUS*

These two French works are thought to have been written just after 1200. The Didot-*Perceval*, also known as the Prose Perceval, generally follows Perceval's adventures as related by Chrétien and in the Second Continuation and adds exploits that lead to his completion of the Grail Quest. Its later parts switch to accounts of Arthur's accomplishments and tragedies. Merlin is involved more here than in any other Grail romance outside of de Boron, and there is a curious emphasis on the Grail knight wearing the color red.

Perlesvaus, though longer, more complex, and considered a greater literary achievement, also begins with a rehash of Chrétien (albeit with a change in the name of the protagonist to Perlesvaus) and triumphant completion of the Grail Quest, and then similarly switches to tales of Arthur and Guinevere, their son Loholt, and the foibles and redemption of Lancelot, who, the anonymous author states, failed the Grail Quest because of his affair with Guinevere.

THE VULGATE CYCLE

Dating from around 1215-1235, the three romances that make up the Vulgate Cycle are most significant for having been the main source for Malory's *Le Morte D'Arthur*. The three are linked because they are thought to have been planned out by the same anonymous writer. That writer is widely believed to have been responsible for all or most of the first part, known as the "Lancelot Propre." However, most scholars, according to Lacy in *The Arthurian Handbook*, believe other authors wrote the following *La Queste del saint Graal* and *La Mort Artu*, though they followed the outlines laid down by the cycle's architect.

The entire Vulgate Cycle, which Lacy calls "intrinsically valuable for its vision, scope, and technique," is largely responsible for ideals of chivalry and courtly love as expressed in Malory and much subsequent Arthurian literature. The author of *Le Morte D'Arthur* drew mainly on elements in the *Queste* and the *Mort Artu*.

The *Queste* makes it Galahad who completes the Grail Quest. After recounting the attempts of Perceval, Gauvain, Lionel, Hector and Bors, the story tells how Galahad, not only related to the Grail Kings but also descended from King David, possessed special powers that enabled him to complete the sacred task. Drawing on Chrétien, the Continuations, de Boron, and other previous literature, the *Queste* presents many of the most familiar Arthurian features, including the Sword in the Stone, the Perilous Seat, and the sense of a Christian-based struggle against evil. However, the Bleeding Lance and Broken Sword of earlier tales are transformed into the lance of Longinus (which pierced the side of Christ on the cross) and King David's sword. And the Grail, instead of being the cup from which Christ drank, is the vessel from which he and his disciples ate the paschal lamb.

The *Mort Artu*, continuing the story told in the *Queste*, presents several other famous features – the split between Arthur and Lancelot, the betrayal of Arthur by his nephew Mordred, Arthur's mortal wound suffered while killing Mordred in battle, the throwing of Excalibur into the lake (where it is received by the hand of the Lady of the Lake), and the bearing of Arthur's body out to sea, accompanied by Morgain and her enchanted attendants.

Two other works, *Estoire del saint Graal* and yet another *Merlin*, are often included as part of the Vulgate Cycle, though they are not thought to have been planned by the Cycle's "architect." And there are many other 13th Century Grail romances – among them the Post-Vulgate Cycle and the Prose *Lancelot* – but they do not concern us here. Of more importance are the findings and theories of scholars who studied these early Grail manuscripts, particularly those whose insights laid the way for the eventual solving of the mystery of the legend's true origin

PART TWO:
INVESTIGATING THE MYSTERY:
PREVIOUS DETECTIVE WORK

GRAIL SCHOLARS AND THEORIES: THE CELTIC CONNECTION AND BEYOND

Like murder mysteries, the Grail mystery has its detectives. Coincidentally, modern criminal detective work developed and matured around the same time (the late 19th Century) that Arthurian scholarship flourished and attempted to unravel the origins of the medieval romances, including those of the Grail legend.

This renaissance of interest in all things Arthurian began primarily with Tennyson's *Idylls of the King*, published in 1859. Like Wagner's opera *Parsifal* (1882), which augmented the fresh fascination with the Grail legend, the section of *Idylls* dealing with the icon was sweepingly poetic and feverishly fanciful. Besides influencing subsequent retellings – all the poems, novels, plays and movies to come – these two works also encouraged certain curious minds to attempt a deeper understanding of the original romances' meaning and history.

As a result, 12th and 13th Century manuscripts would be examined and interpreted to a far greater extent than they ever had been before. This new scholarship would strip away the extraneous material that had become attached to the original story, straighten out the chronology and authorship of the early manuscripts, strongly indicate the role of Celtic mythology, and excavate history for the true origins of the Grail tradition.

The Golden Age of Grail scholarship (which primarily occurred in Germany, Britain and the United States) can be roughly dated between 1888, when Alfred Nutt's landmark *Studies on the Legend of the Holy Grail* was published, and 1927, the year Roger Sherman Loomis' *Celtic Myth and Arthurian Romance* appeared. Other significant examinations of the legend and other Arthurian literature during this era included John Rhys' *Studies in the Arthurian Legend*, W.A. Nitze's *Perceval and the Legend of the Holy Grail* and Jessie L. Weston's *From Ritual to Romance*.

GETTING TO THE NUTT OF THE MATTER

Alfred Nutt's *Studies on the Legend of the Holy Grail* was so comprehensive, courageous and insightful that it virtually revolutionized Arthurian scholarship. It was generous and fair as well: Nutt's book included a "Sketch of the Literature Connected with the Grail Cycle" that summarized the views of several previous scholars (both English and Continental), ranging from an examination of La Villemarqué's early contention of a Celtic basis for the Grail legend to discussions of Christian-origin writers Birch-Hirschfield and Albert Schultz that challenged their views without dismissing or scorning them.

Nutt also suggested corrections to authorship and chronology of the early manuscripts, as well as proposing that Wolfram's *Parzival* had been essentially influenced by Chrétien rather than the probably fictional "Kyot," the German author named as his source. He pointed out the fruitful relationship between Irish folklore and the legend. And he divided the Grail stories into two types, the "feud quest" and the "unspelling quest."

Though Nutt did not believe the various stories could be traced back to a single source, "an orderly and logical original," he did conclude they originated in Celtic myth and in other European stories concerning the adventures of a naive yet gifted "Great Fool." He proposed two influential theories about the Grail's connection to Celtic myth:

1) The Grail, in its earliest form, was the Celtic cauldron of regeneration found in many Celtic tales, and

2) The knight or would-be knight's visit to the Grail Castle originally constituted a journey to the Celtic Otherworld.

The Grail became a Christian icon, Nutt surmised, only after medieval authors attached it to Joseph of Arimathea.

LOOMIS ON THE CELTIC GRAIL CONNECTION

The Celtic Grail connection suggested by Nutt and others was most notably summarized and expanded by Roger Sherman Loomis. Born in Japan and educated at Williams, Harvard and Oxford, he taught medieval literature at Columbia and authored more than 20 books.

In his 1927 classic *Celtic Myth and Arthurian Romance* and the later, more widely read *The Grail: From Celtic Myth to Christian Symbol*, Loomis so strongly espoused the Celtic sources of the Grail legend that he often irked other scholars. As Norris J. Lacy wrote in *The Arthurian Encyclopedia*, "he refined his positions, adding or discarding facts and modifying interpretations," but remaining an ardent – he said "pugnacious" – champion of Celtic theories. His books and ideas provoked controversy (often heated), both because a good many scholars thought the ideas themselves radical or even fanciful and because Loomis sometimes pushed them to limits that even he eventually considered rash.

In the preface to *The Grail: From Celtic Myth to Christian Symbol*, Loomis began by admitting that he had pulled back from some of the assertions in earlier books and papers on the subject, but he made it clear that his central position was unwavering. "For what," he asked, "is more likely than that an important branch of Arthurian literature should have first arisen in what has been called the Celtic Fringe in the Dark Ages as a medley of semi-pagan traditions, and that it should have gradually been rationalized and Christianized in conformity with the tastes and beliefs of French and Anglo-Norman society."

Loomis goes on to say that this is exactly "what one would expect to happen to a Celtic vessel of plenty: at first, a thing of mere magic, it would become in time possessed of miraculous and sacred powers, and emerge at last a Christian symbol."

CAULDRONS AND OTHER MAGIC VESSELS

"[I]n nearly all mythologies," wrote Jung and von Franz, "there is a miraculous vessel... Often, especially as a cooking pot, it effects transformation."

No mythology is richer in magic cauldrons and wonder-working vessels than that of the Celts. And it is these, as Nutt, Loomis and other scholars have indicated, that offer some of the most compelling clues regarding the Grail legend.

Geoffrey Ashe points out in *King Arthur's Avalon: The Story of Glastonbury* that "the word 'grail' signifies a vessel, generally a deep dish, though its application to a cup raises no difficulty. Fanciful derivations given by weavers of romance need not detain us. The conception of *the* Grail, one must reiterate – the dish or bowl or goblet *par excellence* – is not originally Christian at all. Wonder-working vessels confront us in British literature long before there is any allusion to the chalice of Christ... At the bottom of the business lies a stratum of Celtic fable about a miraculous cauldron."

Following a similar train of thought, Jung and von Franz cite "a few vessels from Celtic legends which exhibit a more or less close relation to the Grail story."

Among these are Bran's magic vessel, the cauldron of Caridwen, which "contained a beverage of wisdom and inspiration." Bran is a particularly intriguing character in regard to the Grail legend. He suffered a wound that would not heal, very much like the ailment of the Fisher King. And a figure with a similar name, Bron, is designated the Grail-guarding "Rich Fisher" in De Boron's *Joseph of Arimathea*.

There is also the cauldron at Tyrnog and the vessel mentioned in "Preiddeu Annwn" ("The Spoils of the Underworld"), one of the Thirteen Treasures of the Isle of Britain, which has similar properties. "If meat were put in it to boil for a coward, it would never be boiled. But if meat were put in it for a brave man, it would be boiled forthwith." Never mind that a brave man might deserve a nice grilled tenderloin instead. Jung and von Franz find this attribute "in many ways suggestive of the Grail," as does Loomis, who suspects that it is the source of the Grail's ability to discriminate "between the worthy and the unworthy" in some of the later romances, such as the First Continuation of *Le Conte du Graal*, where Gawain is denied sustenance from it because he failed to show proper humility at one point.

There are several other Celtic cauldrons of interest, including the muses-producing cauldron of Ogyvran the Giant, the cauldron captured by Cúchulainn from the King of the Shadowy City, and the one snared by Arthur from the chief of Hades, recounted in Taliesin's *The Spoils of Annwn*.

In *The Woman's Encyclopedia of Myths and Secrets*, Barbara Walker writes: "Among the Celts of Gaul and Britain, the Cauldron of Regeneration was the central religious mystery..." She notes that the Irish goddess Badb's name means "boiling" and that she was "the producer of life, wisdom, inspiration, and enlightenment. To Welsh bards she was the Goddess Branwen..., owner of the Cauldron of Regeneration in which dead men could be resuscitated overnight. As 'a powerful fairy queen,' the Lady of the Lake of the Basin, she dwelt in a sacred lake from which her brother Bran the Blessed raised the cauldron later known as the Holy Grail [here Walker is making an assumptive connection that many Grail scholars make]. This pagan god was Christianized as Bron, alleged brother-in-law of Joseph of

Arimathea, who was supposed to have brought the Grail to Britain. Actually, the Grail was well established in British paganism long before its legend was assimilated to that of Christ."

We will also meet Bron (aka Brons) in a later chapter on the connection between fish mythology, the Grail and *Amanita muscaria*, where we will see that he places a fish and the Grail together in Robert de Boron's *Joseph of Arimathea*.

We will also see how the shamanic practices of the Celtic druids prove suggestive in solving the mystery of the Grail legend's origin. But the greatest source of clues boils in those cauldrons – particularly one.

MAGICAL POTION OF INSPIRATION AND KNOWLEDGE

The most intriguing Celtic story of a magic vessel, for the purposes of our investigation, is that of the Cauldron of Cerridwen (a more common spelling than Jung and von Franz's "Carwidwen") and the child Gwion.

Here is how Robert Graves relates the tale in *The White Goddess*.

Hoping to cure her deformed son Morfran, Cerridwen "boiled up a cauldron of inspiration and knowledge, which had to be kept on the simmer for a year and a day. Season by season, she added to the brew magical herbs gathered in their correct planetary hours. While she gathered the herbs she put little Gwion... to stir the cauldron. Towards the end of the year three burning drops flew out and fell on little Gwion's finger. He thrust it into his mouth and at once understood the nature and meaning of all things past, present and future..."

The magical potion also enabled Gwion to transform his appearance, which came in handy when he attempted to escape the angered Cerridwen. He changed into such forms as a hare, a fish and a bird (paralleling, as we shall see, the drug-imbued shaman's shape-shifting hallucinations). All seemed lost after he changed to a grain of wheat, because Cerridwen swallowed him. However, this resulted in one final transformation: Cerridwen became pregnant from the grain. Nine months later she gave birth to Taliesen, the divinely inspired poet of Wales.

The Gwion story bears a striking resemblance to another notable Celtic legend about the famous Irish figure Finn Mac Cool (also spelled Mac Coul and Mac Cumhaill).

In the story of Finn and the Salmon of Wisdom Mac Cool is left to tend a very special salmon that is cooking over a fire. When he accidentally touches the fish he experiences something very similar to what befell Gwion. Celtic scholar Jean Markale, in his *Grail: The Celtic Origins of the Sacred Icon*, called this tale nothing less than "the key to the Grail Quest." Indeed, we will see how it has great significance regarding my solution to the Grail mystery in a later chapter.

ENTER MISS WESTON

Late in life Roger Sherman Loomis disavowed certain chapters of *Celtic Myth and Arthurian Romance*, saying that he "retracted in particular my adherence to Dr. Jessie Weston's ingenious hypothesis concerning the Grail and Lance, for lack of valid and clearly pertinent evidence."

The hypothesis to which he refers is presented in Weston's *From Ritual to Romance*, initially published in 1920. That work looms above even Loomis' and all other Grail scholars' books for several reasons, not least of which is its influence on what is widely accepted as the most significant poem of the 20th Century, T.S. Eliot's *The Waste Land* (an influence that Eliot makes clear in the footnotes to that classic).

Loomis' view of Weston is typical of authors who write about the Grail legend. Most, if they mention her at all, tend to couch vaguely reasoned dismissal within a cushion of faint praise. Or even not so faint. Geoffrey Ashe, for example, wrote in *King Arthur's Avalon*: "Miss Weston's elucidation of the Grail, as far as it goes, is an immortal feat of scholarship. Her account of the way her story grew is perhaps less convincing. As a matter of fact neither she nor those who agree with her have made themselves entirely clear." And then Ashe, like so many others who've discussed Weston, refuses to make himself clear about what he finds wrong with her theories.

This belittling attitude is curious, because Weston's assertions, though somewhat radical, have never been disproved. One cannot help but suspect that this curious attitude toward *From Ritual to*

Romance is due to jealousy of the book's popularity and the bold thrust of its theories – as well as Victorian/Edwardian revulsion at Weston's insertion of the nasty subject of sex into previously pristine Arthurian scholarship.

This dismissal, as we shall see in the next chapter, is undeserved. In fact, of all the Grail detectives, Weston came closest to solving the mystery of the legend's true origin. Her intuitive speculations will lead us to the most satisfying answer yet.

THE GREATEST GRAIL DETECTIVE ALMOST SOLVES THE MYSTERY

Not only the title, but the plan and a good deal of the incidental symbolism of the poem were suggested by Miss Jessie L. Weston's book on the Grail legend: From Ritual to Romance *(Cambridge). Indeed, so deeply am I indebted, Miss Weston's book will elucidate the difficulties of the poem much better than my notes can do; and I recommend it (apart from the great interest of the book itself) to any who think such elucidation of the poem worth the trouble.*

T.S. Eliot, "Notes on The Waste Land"

Besides profoundly influencing what may be the greatest poem of the 20th century, Jessie Laidlaw Weston's *From Ritual to Romance* came closer to solving the mystery of the Grail legend than any other book before or since – until the one you are now reading. And my book, from a certain point of view, simply completes the quest that Weston initiated in her final and finest work. (Of course, that does not mean that she would have approved of my theories.)

In *From Ritual to Romance*, published a year before the appearance of *The Waste Land*, Weston proved herself the Miss Marple of Grail detectives.

Like most contemporary and subsequent scholars who wrote of the Grail legend, Weston saw a strong connection with Celtic mythology. However, she also believed that the origins of the legend ranged even further back in history and across continents.

Weston (1850-1928) first became involved with the history of the Grail as a highly regarded translator of Arthurian literature into modern English from Old French, Middle English and Middle High German. However, she eventually began to write theoretical works, culminating with her imaginative view of the Grail legend. For her, the solution to the mystery of the Holy Grail resided in the mystery religions of the eastern Mediterranean and the Middle East.

Weston speculated that the Grail legend contained remnants of secret traditions dating back to ancient cultic practices, and this view alienated many of her fellow scholars. However, she has had her admirers beyond Eliot. The eminent Arthurian expert Geoffrey Ashe once wrote that "Miss Weston's elucidation of the Grail, as far as it goes, is an immortal feat of scholarship... As Miss Weston proves – and her whole theory of the Grail turns on this – the pervading stress is on the Divine Presence, on the Sacramental Meal, on the Bread of Life..." It must also be noted, though, that Ashe believed Weston had not been clear enough and that her theories had not held up well, though he doesn't explain his reasons for thinking so.

Had Ashe, like others who appreciated Weston, but not nearly enough, realized the significance of her linking of the Grail procession with what she calls the mystery religions' "Mystic Meal," he might have figured out himself where the secret of the Grail lies.

AN INTUITIVE AIM

Like many other literary scholars and cultural anthropologists of her time, Weston became excited and deeply influenced by Sir James G. Frazer's *The Golden Bough*, published in several volumes between 1911 and 1915. Frazer's comprehensive and brilliantly (if not always accurately) interpretive collection of folklore and mythology, with its detailed descriptions of religious rituals around the world, largely shaped her Grail hypothesis.

From Ritual to Romance encompassed Frazer, recent discoveries in cultural anthropology and religious history, and Weston's own thorough knowledge of Arthurian literature. Perhaps more importantly, it drew upon her intuition.

Though artfully written, Weston's book is a somewhat difficult work, challenging the reader to keep up at several turns. But it is worth the trouble for the way it shoots like a well-aimed arrow straight and true toward the heart of the Grail mystery, and very nearly solves it. Basically, her theory revolved around her belief that:

"The Grail Story is not... the product of imagination, literary or popular. At its root lies the record, more or less distorted, of an ancient Ritual, having for its ultimate object the initiation into the secret of Life, physical and spiritual."

Like many fellow Grail scholars, Weston found important clues in the fossil-field of Celtic myth. She acknowledged how the French and other European Grail romances that began to appear in the late 12th Century were derived from Celtic sources, brought to France by the Normans, who had invaded Britain a century before.

However, Weston also believed that the trail led farther back – much farther. Several features of the Grail legend, she asserted, related to elements of the Mystery Religions of Greece and the Middle East, to the rites of the peoples who celebrated the death and rebirth of vegetation gods like Attis, Tammuz and Mithra, and to the fish symbolism that is strangely widespread throughout world mythology – and to the Soma ritual of Vedic India. As we shall see in later chapters, these last two routes lead to highly significant clues.

There is a tendency among critics of Weston's approach, often labeled either the "ritual theory" or "vegetation theory," to dismiss it as eccentrically isolated. This simply was not true. Other scholars around the turn of the century and just before – W.E. Nitze, for instance – were looking in the same direction, and their work, along with Frazer's *The Golden Bough*, influenced hers.

Providing a sense of how prevalent this Frazer-based view of the Grail legend was at the time is the entry on the Grail in the famous Eleventh Edition of the *Encyclopedia Britannica* (1910-11) that reads, in part:

"The researches of Professor Mannhardt in Germany and J.G. Frazer in England have amply demonstrated the enduring influence exercised on popular thought and custom by certain primitive forms of vegetation worship, of which the most noteworthy example is the so-called mysteries of Adonis. Here the ordinary processes of nature and progression of the seasons were symbolized under the figure of the death and resuscitation of the god. These rites are found all over the world, and in his monumental work, *The Golden Bough*, Dr. Frazer has traced a host of extant beliefs and practices to this source. The earliest form of the Grail story, the Gawain-Bleheris version, exhibits a marked affinity with the characteristic features of the Adonis or Tammuz worship; we have a castle on the sea-shore, a dead body on a bier, the identity of which is never revealed, mourned over with solemn rites; a wasted country, whose desolation is mysteriously connected with the dead man, and which is restored to fruitfulness when the quester asks the meaning of the marvels he beholds (the two features of the weeping women and the wasted land being retained in versions where they have no significance); finally the mysterious food-providing, self-acting talisman of a common feast – one and all of these features may be explained as survivals of the Adonis ritual."

THE MYSTIC MEAL

"[T]o the romance writers the Grail was something secret, mysterious and awful, the exact knowledge of which was reserved to a select few," Weston noted in a chapter of *From Ritual to Romance* titled "The Secret of the Grail."

It is a distinct possibility, Weston argued, that this solemnly sacred atmosphere is due to the Grail legend being part of a long, closely guarded ritual tradition – one that could be traced back at least as far as the mystery cults of the Mediterranean region.

Weston believed the religious practices of these various cults had a common bond, and that the Grail legend is one legacy of this central element. The characters and incidents of the legend, she wrote, are "fragments of a once widespread Nature Cult," whose object was "the attainment of union with the god, by way of ecstasy."

Drawing upon the *The Golden Bough,* Weston wrote that "parallel and over-lapping forms of this cult, the name of the god, and certain details of the ritual may differ in different countries, but whether he hails from Babylon, Phrygia, or Phoenicia, whether he be called Tammuz, Attis, or Adonis, the main lines of the story are fixed, and invariable. Always he is young and beautiful, always the beloved of a great goddess, always he is the victim of a tragic and untimely death, a death which entails bitter loss and misfortune upon a mourning world, and which, for the salvation of that world, is followed by a resurrection. Death and resurrection, mourning and rejoicing, present themselves in sharp antithesis in each and all of the forms."

One of the features shared by the Grail legend and these other myths is the Mystic Meal. In the mysteries celebrating the Phrygian god Attis, for example, "the first and most important point was a Mystic Meal, at which the food partaken of was served in the sacred vessels."

Weston found the connection obvious: "Now is it not clear that we have here a close parallel with the Grail romances?"

What could certainly be described as a Mystic Meal forms the most important episode in the earliest of the Grail stories, Chrétien de Troyes' *Le Conte du Graal* (Perceval) – the processional feast at the Fisher King's castle. Similar scenes take place in other early Grail romances, including Wolfram von Eschenbach's German *Parzival.*

Other Grail scholars have also emphasized the importance of the ritual-feast element in the Grail stories. Richard Cavendish in *King Arthur and the Grail* writes:

"What is clear is that the Grail is connected with food. It carries the Mass-wafer that is the only nourishment of the aged Grail King and it is associated with the fine feast that Perceval and the Fisher King enjoy. It does not serve the feast [in *Le Conte du Graal*], as it does in many of the other stories, but it passes before Perceval's eyes with each course of the banquet. The connection with food, and with especially enjoyable and satisfying food, is one of the Grail's most constant characteristics in the stories."

Cavendish then notes that the Grail legend is part of a long line of mythology involving what he calls "the otherworld banquet" in Celtic and other traditions. "Feasting was one of the principal pleasures of the otherworld, and the variety of vessels which provided the otherworld banquet – cauldrons, cups, drinking-horns, platters – probably has much to do with the later variations in the shape of the Grail...

"Just as the food and drink of mortals supports human life, so in mythology the food and drink of the otherworld supports the immortal life and eternal youth of its inhabitants. Zeus and the Greek gods lived on the nectar and ambrosia of immortality. The Norse gods ate the apples of Idun, which kept them forever young. The Irish god Goibniu brewed beer in a cauldron for the otherworld feast which preserved the Tuatha De Danann, the Irish deities, from ageing and death. The Dagda's inexhaustible cauldron could bring the dead back to life. Another Irish god, Midir, had a similar cauldron, which was stolen from him by the hero Cúchulainn. The Welsh god Bran owned a cauldron which reanimated dead warriors who were placed in it."

While the Grail and what it contains is part of this tradition, it is something more than food – even the "usual" otherworldly food. As Cavendish says: "It is difficult to resist the conclusion that the light of the Grail is the radiance of the Divine Presence...."

Weston traced these Mystic Meals of many mythologies back to the oldest sacred feast mentioned in sacred literature – the Soma ceremony that plays an important role in the most ancient of Hindu scriptures, the *Rig-Veda*.

If Weston had known what Soma actually was, she might have solved the mystery of the Grail. Even without that knowledge, she came very close.

THE MEDICINE MAN

In a key chapter midway through *From Ritual to Romance* titled "The Medicine Man," Weston becomes intrigued by 23 verses from the *Rig-Veda* (beginning at 10.97) that she found quoted in German scholar Leopold von Schroeder's *Mysterium und Mimus im Rig-Veda* (1908). This section of the Hindu text presents "a monologue placed in the mouth of a Doctor, or Medicine Man, who vaunts the virtue of his herbs, and their power to cure human ills."

The healer begins by praising a wide variety of "ancient herbs," calling them "you divine ones." Then he focuses on one herb he finds superior to all the rest:

In Soma's realm are many herbs,

And knowledge a hundredfold have they,

Of all these herbs thou art the best

The wish to fulfill and heart to heal.

He then calls on "all you herbs in Soma's kingdom" to "give to this herb all your strength." The herbs answer:

That man [the ill and apparently special patient] *to whom a Brahman gives us,*

Him shall we save from harm, O King.

Weston surmises this means that the Doctor "is obviously a Brahmin, and the Medicine Man here, as elsewhere, unites the function of Priest and Healer."

Professor von Schroeder, Weston notes, suggested that "this Dramatic Monologue formed part of the ceremonies of a Soma feast, that it is the Soma plant from which the heavenly drink is brewed which is to be understood as the first of all herbs and the curer of all ills, and the reference to Soma as the King of the herbs seems to bear out this suggestion."

Weston sees a relationship between this *Rig-Veda* healer/priest and what we know now as the shamanic tradition (though she does not use the word "shaman"). She finds it present in fertility ceremonies around the world, particularly in Greek "figures in a Religious Mystery, the God who every year is born, and dies, and rises again; his Mother and his Bride; the Antagonist who kills him; the Medicine Man who restores him to life." And she sees the Brahmin's role as "identical with that assigned to his modern counterpart, i.e., that of restoring to life or health the slain, or suffering, representative of the Vegetation Spirit."

And, finally, she asserts "that the presence of such a character in the original ritual drama of Revival...underlies the romantic form of the Grail legend..."

SIR GAWAIN AND THE HEALING 'HERB'

In the deep, dim background of the Grail's much-touted curative qualities lies an original, shamanic ritual involving some very real, earthly substance with healing powers, Weston sensed. However, this substance also contained other properties, perhaps dangerous and/or sacred ones, which caused the tellers of the tale to cloak its identity in layers of mystery.

As a result, by the time the early Grail romances were written almost all direct references to healers or healing agents had been expunged from the legend. Yet Weston did find one passage that she considered revelatory in this regard. And she found it in the very first Grail manuscript – Chrétien's *Le Conte du Graal.*

This passage, however, doesn't concern Perceval. It appears in the section dealing with Gawain – the part of Chrétien's story that has puzzled so many scholars because it seems so unrelated to the rest.

Gawain comes upon a wounded knight lying by the roadside, and we are told that he possesses knowledge of an extraordinary healing agent, which he finds nearby.

Of wounds and healing lore

Did Sir Gawain know more

Than any man alive.

To make the sick knight thrive,

A herb to cure all pain

That in a hedge had lain

He spied, and thence he plucked it.

Weston also quotes a nearly identical passage from Wolfram's *Parzival*:

Of wounds and healing lore
Had Sir Gawain learned more
Than any other knew.
Within a hedge there grew
A herb he long had known
By his master he'd been shown
And taught its healing spell,
And so he knew it well.

Weston notes there are references to Gawain's healing abilities in a few other medieval texts, such as a Dutch *Perceval* and the French poem *Lancelot et le Cerf au pied blanc*, though she admits these may have simply been borrowings from Chrétien's earlier work.

Nevertheless, Weston believed she may have discovered in these few lines the key to the way the ur-story of the Grail legend ended long before it became buried in ambiguity. She'd found, in fact, the key to the true nature of the Grail itself.

AN ANCIENT SECRET

At the end of her chapter "The Medicine Man" in *From Ritual to Romance*, Weston provides the most intriguing and cogent solution – or, at least, near-solution – to the mystery of the Grail legend ever given.

"No other knight, save Gawain, has the reputation of a Healer, yet Gawain, the Maidens' Knight, the 'fair Father of Nurture' is, at first sight, hardly the personage one might expect to possess such a skill. Why he should be so persistently connected with healing was for long a problem to me; recently, however, I have begun to suspect that we have in this apparently motiveless attribution the survival of an early stage of tradition in which not only did Gawain cure the Grail King, but he did so, not be means of a question, or by the welding of a broken sword, but by more obvious and natural means, the administration of a healing herb."

From this and other evidence Weston concludes that the Grail legend belongs to a mythic-magical tradition revolving around the ritual curing or resurrection of a royal or godly figure – the Fisher King in the Grail story and such figures as the vegetation gods Attis, Adonis and Mithra in others. All such myths, she believes, disguise an ancient secret involving a very real healing substance.

She ends "The Medicine Man" with the declaration that "the *mise-en-scene* of the Grail story was originally a loan from a ritual actually performed, and familiar to those who first told the tale. This ritual, in its earlier stages comparatively simple and objective in form, under the process of an insistence upon the inner and spiritual significance, took upon itself a more complex and esoteric character, the rite became a Mystery, and with this change the *role* of the principal actors became of heightened significance. That of the Healer could no longer be adequately fulfilled by the administration of a medicinal remedy; the relation of Body and Soul became of cardinal importance for the Drama, the Medicine Man gave place to the Redeemer; and his task involved more than the administration of the original Herbal remedy."

Weston does not quit there. Still to come in *From Ritual to Romance* are more fascinating findings and intriguing insights – particularly in the chapters "The Fisher King," "The Secret of the Grail" and "The Perilous Chapel" – and we will return to consider these.

However, her speculations in "The Medicine Man" are sufficient to launch a fresh examination of the relationship between the Grail legend and its probable shamanistic roots. For it is in the role and practices of the ancient shaman – and in the Celtic myths and legends that resulted from storytelling by and about shamans – that the true secret of the Grail is hidden, ready to be revealed at last.

PART THREE:
THE KEY TO THE PUZZLE – SHAMANISM

THE SHAMAN AND THE OTHERWORLD

The shaman's activity is based on ideas of space, and although the everyday world is permeated by spirits there are also other, separate realms to which shamans must travel... to persuade [the spirits] to behave differently...

The gulf in space [can] sometimes reflect the moral inferiority of humans as they live a degraded existence in a state of separation from the divine. In this light, the shaman's journey resembles the quest in other, more explicitly moralistic religious systems, such as the search for the Holy Grail. It is possible to see this as a quest to return to some primordial state of grace. The shaman is a specialist in crossing this otherwise impassable gulf, and only a shaman has the necessary technique and courage to do so.

Piers Vitebsky, *The Shaman*

The Grail legend springs from the secrets of ancient shamans. Shamanism, in fact, lies at the root of much Western literature and other arts. A connection between epic literature and the practices of the shaman was proposed in no less a work than Mircea Eliade's *Shamanism: Archaic Techniques of Ecstasy*. Published in 1951, this classic remains the most respected and influential study of the subject.

At the end of *Shamanism*, in his Epilogue, Eliade muses over "the likenesses between the accounts of shamanic ecstasies and certain epic themes in oral literature. The shaman's adventures in the other world, the ordeals that he undergoes in his ecstatic descents below and ascents to the sky, suggest the adventures of the figures in popular tales and the heroes of epic literature. Probably a large number of epic 'subjects' or motifs, as well as many characters, images, and clichés of epic literature, are, finally, of ecstatic origin, in the sense that they were borrowed from the narratives of shamans describing their journeys and adventures in the superhuman worlds."

Some modern scholars have found strong shamanic strains in Celtic mythology and in the Grail legend. However, to comprehend these associations it is necessary to have a basic understanding of what shamanism is. Again, Eliade is the best source for an introduction.

CLASSIC SHAMANISM AND THE 'TECHNIQUE OF ECSTASY'

After warning against the too-wide application of the term to include every sort of healer, magician and sorcerer (an application that became something of a garden industry three decades after Shamanism appeared), Eliade explains that shamanism "in the strict sense is pre-eminently a religious phenomenon of Siberia and Central Asia. The word comes to us, through the Russian, from the Tungus word *saman*... [T]hrough this whole region in which the ecstatic experience is considered the religious experience par excellence, the shaman, and he alone, is the great master of ecstasy. A first definition of the complex phenomenon, and perhaps the least hazardous, will be shamanism = *technique of ecstasy* [italics Eliade's]."

The shaman is his people's "medicine man," spiritual counselor, historian, storyteller, poet and much else. Central to his functions is the trance, which he achieves through means that may involve some or all of the following – drumming, dancing, chanting, singing and the ingestion of hallucinogens. The shaman, states Eliade, "specializes in a trance during which his soul is believed to leave his body and ascend to the sky or descend to the underworld."

Though shamanism takes its most ancient and classic forms in areas of Asia that have long been a part of Russia, it has also existed for innumerable centuries in many other places. Eliade himself documents shamanic practices in North and South America, Australia, Borneo, Sumatra, Malaysia, Polynesia and several other far-flung places. He also devotes sections of his book to "Shamanic Ideologies and Techniques among the Indo-Europeans" and "Shamanic Symbolisms and Techniques in Tibet, China, and the Far East."

Though Eliade only briefly mentions Celtic shamanism, several other subsequent scholars have detailed the clear shamanic characteristics of the Celts' spiritual leaders, the druids. Because Celtic tribes were able to retreat to regions – Ireland, Scotland and Wales – that were the last to be conquered by Roman, Christian or other more "civilized" peoples. Due to this special longevity, Celtic lore and myth preserves particularly vivid shamanic components.

A FIRE IN THE HEAD

"In Celtic lands a strong belief in the immanence of the Otherworld persists even today," Tom Cowan writes in *Fire in the Head: Shamanism and the Celtic Spirit*, the most exhaustive study of Celtic shamanism to date. "Modern Irish storytelling abounds with ordinary people who hear the songs and merriment of the faery folk, encounter troupes of faeries, and slip into the twilight of the Otherworld, where they undergo adventures that rival the accounts of the greatest shamans."

Cowan states that the "vestiges of Celtic shamanism, fragmented though they are, shine bright and clear, for the Celtic spirit and personality is a fertile breeding ground for shamanic experiences." Noting Mircea Eliade's belief "that the material that becomes a culture's mythology is derived in part from the journeys of historical shamans into the Otherworld," Cowan asserts that many of the Irish and other Celtic deities and heroes are so derived, with some of these bigger-than-life figures representing "historic shamans themselves possibly based on their journeys into nonordinary reality."

The great mythic warrior-hero Cúchulainn, for example, "suffered a faery sickness as part of his introduction into the Otherworld" that is reminiscent of the fact that "the man or woman being initiated into shamanic mysteries commonly suffers a debilitating illness during which he or she has the first meaningful encounter with spirits who use the delirium or coma to introduce the aspirant to the shamanic state of consciousness."

But it is in the adventures of Finn MacCool that Cowan particularly finds "shamanic features."

Much like Perceval, Finn is brought up in the woods by his mother, who shelters him there because she fears attempts on his life. There the young man learns "the secrets of magic and nature" and eventually studies at the foot of wise old Finegas. As we shall see, the way Finn receives universal wisdom from tasting merely the tiniest portion of the Salmon of Knowledge, caught after many years of trying by Finegas, relates revealingly to the secret origin of the Grail legend.

MEN OF THE OAK

The druids were closely associated with one of the kinds of trees that grow in symbiosis with *Amanita muscaria*. Observing that druids always employed oak leaves in their rituals, the Roman writer Pliny became the first historian to associate druid with the Greek word for oak, drus. The word "druid" has subsequently been considered to mean "men of the oak," "having knowledge of the oak," or something similar.

Druids and other Celts revered not only the oak but nature in general, and particularly the forests. Celtic scholar Barry Cunliffe asserts that "the essence of Celtic religion" is making sacrifices to the gods and spirits of the woods. Cowan notes the similarity between the Celtic word for oak, *dur*, and the one for door, *duir*, and he quotes an unnamed immigrant from Ireland to the United States about the significance of the oak: "The oak is the doorway between the worlds. It's the tree of life, the oak. That is a part of our culture and the tree is something you climb up to go to another world."

Like shamans of other cultures and various heroes in Celtic mythology, the druids indulged in shape-shifting – taking the form of various animals important to their culture. The druids, Cowan asserts, "were the archshapeshifters in ancient Celtic culture.... [Their] 'magic sleep' may have been a hypnotic trance similar to the shamanic trance in which they changed their shapes and delved into the deeper, unseen realms of the Otherworld."

THE FENIANS OF THE ENCHANTED FOREST

Ancient Irish mythology is largely divided into two camps – the Ulster Cycle and the Fenian Cycle. Unlike the Ulster tales, which primarily deal with Cúchulainn and the other figures and adventures of the original Irish people, Fenian stories almost always have wild, wooded settings and a sense of the supernatural and the magical about them. They are, Cowan writes, "really about Faeryland." The Fenians' "favorite haunt was the borderland between the worlds of human society and Faerie – the wild, trackless, and enchanted forest."

To become a Fenian, a man had to undergo a series of arduous, initiatory ordeals. These ranged from defending himself from several warriors with just a hazel stick and a shield while being buried to his waist in the ground to memorizing twelve books of poetry. Through these and other tests, he proved himself a worthy mixture of warrior, athlete, poet and magician.

Hunters who lived by their wiles, the Fenians were outsiders who, according to Cowan, "were probably looked upon much like shamans in other societies, marked by some mental or behavioral irregularity – eccentrics by community standards but with personal power and a lifestyle that was admired and respected."

THE WILD MAN OF THE WOODS

Throughout the British Isles there has long been a tradition of "the wild man of the woods," sometimes more specified as "the wild man of the oak woods" – a frightening but also magical figure who roams the forests. Three incarnations of this wild man took in ancient and medieval times were the Green Man, Cernunnos and Merlin.

The Green Man is usually portrayed as a bearded fellow clothed in leaves, vines and other foliage. He represents the savage fecundity and fertility of the woodlands.

Cernunnos is the Horned God who is the most prominent of the mythological personages depicted on the famous Gundestrup Cauldron (housed at the National Museum of Denmark in Copenhagen), an astoundingly detailed Celtic artifact thought to date to the sometime between 200 B.C. and the third century A.D.

Holding a serpent with a ram's head in one hand and a torque in the other, he sits in cross-legged, Buddha-like repose. His head is crowned with long stag antlers. His eyes look out with a mesmerizing gaze. Unlike the other male figures on the cauldron, however, Cernunnos is beardless – a feature that has led some Celticists to see Cernunnos as an androgynous figure. In any case, "he," like the Green Man, displays shamanic characteristics, and he is surrounded by animals of the forest.

The same is so of Merlin – or, at least, of the Merlin we find in some of the medieval manuscripts, and less so (but still to some extent) in the more popularized picture of a cantankerous wizard. In some of his earliest depictions, Merlin is an antler-wearing inhabitant of the forest who sometimes acts wildly. He has a close, friendly, association with all the animals of the forest, and possesses a magical power over many.

These, of course, are among the most noted attributes of shamans around the world. We next take a closer look at Merlin, whom some scholars have considered a possible key to the Grail mystery, despite his only peripheral involvement in the legend.

MERLIN: THE ARTHURIAN SHAMAN

Anyone who has delved into the works of Carl Jung knows how deeply concerned he was with occult traditions, especially alchemy. One might have expected the profoundly influential pioneer of modern psychology to have an interest in the Grail legend as well. He did indeed.

In his only autobiographical book, *Memories, Dreams, Reflections*, Jung wrote:

"The stories of the Grail had been of the greatest importance to me ever since I read them, at the age of 15, for the first time. I had an inkling that a great secret still lay hidden behind those stories."

Why, then, did the father of Jungian psychology make few comments about the Grail beyond relating some fascinating dreams concerning it in *Memories*?

Jung gave his reason in that volume. He refrained from writing extensively on the subject, he said, because his wife Emma had made the study of the Grail "her life's task," and she planned to eventually compile her many lectures and other work regarding the subject into a book. "Had it not been for my unwillingness to intrude upon my wife's field, I would unquestionably have had to include the Grail legend in my studies of alchemy."

This may be the greatest loss in the history of Grail scholarship. Fortunately, though, Emma Jung's findings and speculations on the matter were not lost – though they might have been.

She died in 1955, having never finished her Grail book. Carl was advanced in age himself by this time (he would die six years later) and was involved with other pursuits. He simply did not have the time and energy to gather and edit Emma's Grail work.

However, his most noted protégé and assistant, Marie-Louise von Franz, took it upon herself to put together a book based on Emma's lectures, notes and other material. The result, *The Grail Legend* (listing Emma Jung and von Franz as co-authors), is somewhat scattered and incomplete. But it still holds great value.

Originally published in 1960 in Germany, *The Grail Legend* was translated into English by Andrea Dykes in 1970, a version republished by Sigo Press in 1986. The book's early chapters offer a basic outline of the early Grail stories that is missing from Weston's *From Ritual to Romance*. For that reason and others, *The Grail Legend* is one of the two most readable and trustworthy introductions to the legend currently in print, though perhaps not as easily digested as the other, Cavendish's *King Arthur and the Grail*.

Like Weston, Jung and von Franz eventually indicate (in their book's final five chapters) that the origins of the legend can be traced back to tribal "medicine men." However, they follow this trail not through one of the Grail knights or would-be knights, but through another Arthurian personage – Merlin.

In doing so, Jung and von Franz come – via a differing route – to the same conclusion as Weston's:

At the heart of the Grail legend is a magical healer, a shaman.

WIZARD AND PROPHET

Merlin was actually called Myrddin in the earliest works that refer to him, but the name was changed to Merdinus or Merlinus, and then Merlin, by European authors because of an unpleasant association with *merdus*, the Latin word for feces.

The Merlin we know best is the wizard whose characteristics Malory wrote of in *Le Morte D'Arthur*. Malory derived most of this from the second part of Robert de Boron's trilogy, *Romanz De L'estoire Dou Graal*.

In the second and third sections of that trilogy, *Merlin* and *Perceval*, we find many familiar Arthurian/Grail characters and themes. The first part, *Joseph D'Arimathe*, presents the Grail as it has usually been considered since, as the chalice used by Jesus Christ at the Last Supper.

Robert writes that the cup was given to Pontius Pilate by a Jew, and that Pilate presented it to Joseph of Arimathea when the latter asked permission to take Jesus's body from the cross. He becomes the first Keeper of the Grail, and eventually passes it on the second Keeper, his brother-in-law Bron, who later carries the holy chalice to Britain. The third part of the trilogy tells how Bron's grandson, Perceval, is destined to be the third and final Keeper. This figure of Bron, as we shall see in a subsequent chapter, "The Fisher King and the Fish," offers a key connection between the Grail and *Amanita muscaria*.

The middle *Merlin* part of the trilogy was perhaps, as Cavendish speculates, "designed to explain how it was that the Grail traveled from the Holy Land to Britain and to recount its subsequent history." But all that exists is a fragmentary and inconclusive tale that is more a tangent than a connecting narrative.

Nevertheless, it is in *Merlin* that Malory found several appealing aspects that he worked into *Morte D'Arthur.* Merlin correctly prophesizes the death of the British king Vortigern (aka Vertigier), and after the early death of his successor Pendragon, he becomes counselor to the new king, Uther, who adds his brother's name to become Uther Pendragon.

During Uther's reign, Merlin performs such feats as magically transporting the boulders of Stonehenge from Ireland to Britain. More to our purposes, he also tells Uther about Joseph of Arimathea and the Grail, which apparently has come to Britain but been lost. Merlin directs the King to establish a Round Table at Carduel (Carlisle). Fifty knights are chosen to be seated at this table for a meal at Whitsuntide, with one place left empty.

This place will eventually be occupied, Merlin declares, sometime during the reign of Uther's successor by a knight, as yet unborn, who will have found the Grail.

The story then ends inconclusively with the famous incident of the sword in the stone. Arthur proves his royal legitimacy by extracting it and is proclaimed king.

WILD MAN OF THE FOREST

The oldest extant manuscripts in which Merlin (like Arthur) is first mentioned are Geoffrey of Monmouth's *Historia regum Britanniae* (The History of the Kings of Britain), written around 1135, and the same author's *Vita Merlini* (The Life of Merlin), written in 1148.

Some of the details about Merlin overlap those found in Robert's later account, including how he prophesized the death of King Vortigern (involving two dragons, one red, one white). However, it is the remarkable material in Geoffrey's *Merlin* pointing toward Merlin's shamanic nature that interests Jung and von Franz most in their attempt to get at the heart of the Grail mystery.

Summarizing that work in their chapter "Merlin As Medicine Man and Prophet," they describe how Merlin "withdraws into the forest, away from human society, because he has gone mad from suffering as the result of a battle between the Scots and [his own] Britons... In the forest, Merlin leads the life of a wild animal, and when by chance he is discovered, the emissaries of his sister Ganieda have to soothe him with song and lyre before they can prevail upon him to return to the world of men. At the sight of a crowd of people, his madness breaks out anew. He is released and is once more free to return to the forest."

Merlin states that he wishes to remain in the forest and grants his wife Gwendolina the right to marry another. However, the honeymoon of the lady and her new husband is not to go undisrupted. Merlin shows up at their house "riding a stag and driving a pack-deer before him."

This image may evoke in the reader's mind the figures of Santa Claus and his reindeer, and not without relevance. Several authors have noted the shamanic influences on Santa Claus, and a few have suggested that the ancient shaman's use of the tree-associated *Amanita muscaria* lies at the source of this and other Christmas traditions, including the Christmas tree and its ornaments.

Merlin "calls to Gwendolina, who is much amused at the spectacle. But when her bridegroom appears at the window, Merlin wrenches off the stag's horns and throws them at the head of his rival, whose skull is shattered. He then flees back to the forest on his stag." However, this wild and crazy guy cartoonishly loses his balance while crossing a stream and is captured.

In captivity he makes such a fuss – "in his yearning for the forest [he] loses all joy in life" – that he's set free again. This time, though, his sister builds him a house in the woods "with seventy windows and doors, where he can devote himself to his astronomical observations," and she resides nearby with her servants.

Here his shamanic tendencies increase. "During the summer, Merlin lives in the open; when the winter cold sets in and he can find nothing to eat, he returns to his observatory where, fortified by his sister with food and drink, 'he explores the stars and sings about future happenings.' Later he teaches her to prophesy and extols her as his equal."

As Jung and von Franz note, in this narrative Merlin "appears to have taken on more than a little of the nature of the Druid priest and Celtic bard. Furthermore, he resembles the general type of primitive medicine man and priestly personality. The shaman and the medicine man and the analogous figure, the Celtic Druid, embody, as it were, the type of religious man who, in complete independence and solitude, opens up a direct and personal approach to the collective unconscious for himself and tries to live the predictions of his guardian spirit, i.e. of his unconscious. The result is that he becomes a source of spiritual life for his surroundings. As Mircea Eliade has shown, states of temporary insanity are often an attribute of the shaman and medicine man."

Jung and von Franz's footnote to this last sentence reads: "In *Shamanism*, pp. 25*ff*, Mircea Eliade has shown that this kind of priest-medicine man corresponds to a type that is spread over the whole world and that the aspects and phases of development of his personality correspond, as [C.G.] Jung has shown, to the process of individuation."

Jung and von Franz also identify Merlin with the general mythological figure of "the fool" and with the "archetype of the trickster," who "always appears as a healing figure..."

In their next chapter, "Merlin and the Alchemical Mercurious," the authors of *The Grail Legend* focus on the significance of Merlin's association with the stag, noting the echoes of Celtic myth.

This relationship is something Merlin "also has in common with Mercurious who is often described in alchemical texts as the *cervus fugitivus* (fugitive stag). It is possible, however, that a memory of the Celtic god Kerunnus [aka Cernunnos] – a god, according to [Jean Marx, writing about the famous Celtic artifact, the cup of Gundestrup, which depicts Kerunnus], who underwent a transformation mystery – also survives in this stag symbol. Kerunnus is dismembered and cooked in a bowl (!) in order to arise again, rejuvenated, from the dead; he therefore undergoes a truly alchemical transformation mystery. *In this Merlin would himself be the hidden content of the Grail.*"

MORE RECENT STUDIES OF MERLIN

The mystery of Merlin is more thoroughly investigated in two relatively recent works, Nikolai Tolstoy's *The Quest for Merlin* and Jean Markale's *Merlin: Priest of Nature*, published in France in 1981 and first translated into English in 1995. What these two authors have to say about the subject largely complements the views of Jung and Von Franz and expands upon them. Both illuminate the connections between the Celtic "magician" and the shamanic "technique of ecstasy."

"[T]here is a close relationship between the Celtic bard who achieves prophetic insight through an ecstatic trance or frenzy," Tolstoy writes, "and the comparable practices of shamanism as it has survived in Siberia and elsewhere..." After describing shamanic practices, he goes on to say: "The story of Merlin, as it appears in its variant guises (Myrddin-Lailoken-Suibhne), precisely parallels these aspects of the shaman's 'call' and ecstatic vision. Indeed, the parallel is so precise that it is impossible to doubt that the original Merlin saga comprised the story of a late British shaman-figure."

Tolstoy speculates that there may have been an actual Merlin as late as the sixth century A.D. – a Last of the Druids, or nearly, to whom more ancient Druidic legends and Celtic motifs (such as that of the Trickster) were passed down through the Celtic/British oral tradition, parts of them to be finally set down in writing by Geoffrey and de Boron.

"Behind the darkness of history and cloak of legend, we may dimly perceive a sacred place... At its Centre was Merlin; to be seen as Trickster and Master of Beasts, Lord of the Wild Hunt, psychopomp and devil; and, emerging from the wilderness chaos, the Incarnation of Divinity, Guardian of the Grail, and sacrificial Saviour and Victim."

In his chapter "The Shaman of Hart Fell and the Ritual of Renewal," Tolstoy details further evidence of the shamanic elements found in Celtic myth and particularly in the figure of Merlin.

Merlin and similar Celtic/Nordic figures represented the holy man of prehistoric tribes who fasted, retreated, and "mediated between God and man after their separation." He "wore antlers and skins, and was envisaged as possessing a special relationship with the wild deer... Despite the fact that the earth was stocked with a superfluity of game, primitive man possessed an inspired sense of what would now be termed ecological balance."

One can see how far back this ur-shaman reaches in humanity's history by looking at one of the earliest known examples of human art – the famous "Sorcerer" painting on a wall of the Cave of the Trois-Frères in southwestern France. Dating from approximately 13,000 B.C., it depicts a shaman wearing a deer's head crowned with antler, an owl-like mask, wolf's ears, chamois' beard, bear's claws and a horse's tail.

The next-best-known work of ancient art known to represent a deer-man or deer-god is the previously mentioned figure of Cernunnos on the Gundestrop Cauldron, in the National Museum at Copenhagen. Cernunnos (Jung and von Franz's "Kerunnus") is depicted there as a Celtic god with branching antlers, surrounded by wild beasts, with a stag and wolf most prominent. Of the antler-helmed picture of Merlin drawn by Geoffrey, Tolstoy asserts: "It is hardly possible to have a clearer representation of the Celtic horned god, sometimes known as Cernunnos."

And it is not without significance that this exquisitely wrought work of iron was formed into a cauldron, which might have once been used – like the many other magic cauldrons of Celtic myth – to concoct a brew that would indeed bridge, if only for a few hours, the distance between God and man.

Regarding motifs of the Grail stories, Tolstoy writes: "The most satisfactory explanation of these mysterious symbols derives them from Celtic motifs, and they in turn are bound up inextricably with the story of Merlin and related myths of divine sacrifice."

MARKALE'S *PRIEST OF NATURE*

An even more passionate argument for Merlin as shaman is presented by the noted, colorful French Celtic expert Jean Markale (whose *The Celts: Uncovering the Mythic and Historic Origins of Western Culture* is one of the most widely taught texts on the subject) in his *Merlin: Priest of Nature*.

Many things point to Merlin's shamanic role, in Markale's view, but two in particular affirm it. One, as we have seen, is his intuitive relationship with animals, especially stags. The other is the importance of trees to him.

"In all accounts of him, whatever the circumstances," Markale writes, "one motif dominates the description of Merlin: his special alliance with trees. Above all, Merlin appears as a man of the forest... Merlin occupies a space that is very firm and well defined, and corresponds to the place of the cult of the ancient Celts. It is a sacred space, a sanctuary in the heart of the woods."

Among the trees that would have been most significant for Merlin, besides the apple, Markale notes, were the oak, the birch and the pine. As we have found, the oak was so important to the Celts ("the representation of divinity") that the word "druid" is derived from the word for oak, "drus." The birch was, to many Celts, as it was to Siberians, the "Cosmic Tree," "a tree of life and of immortality." And, writes Markale, "the pine tree is particularly remarkable. It was mentioned by medieval writers because it was a relatively rare species in Britain at the time, and it makes a great deal of sense that it appears as the central pivot of a clearing in a forest – clearings that became places of worship for Celts amid sacred groves.

Not coincidentally, these three trees are the ones most associated with the crimson-topped mushroom that is often found growing beneath them. Merlin is also, Markale states, "a master of plants." Surely he, like shamans before and after him, would have mastered the most magical "plant" of the northern forests. And one reason why he is so linked with the stag is possibly because, as R. Gordon Wasson (profiled in an upcoming chapter) and others have noted, deer and reindeer have a taste for *Amanita muscaria*, and primitive peoples may have first learned of the mushroom's intoxicating properties from observing the way deer stagger about after consuming AM.

Merlin's life in the woods represents, Markale observes, "the rediscovery of an instinctual life." Like other great shamans, he grows into a master who "fires up the mind." Yet he possesses an especially magical quality of a nature almost as transcendent as the Grail, and almost as suggestive of some lost Golden Age. He is, Markale declares, "the madman of the forest, the Wild Man, the master of animals, the sage par excellence, who succeeds in rediscovering the purity of mythical times when humans lived in peace with the lower orders... He represents, in fact, a certain conception of the world and of life. His behavior might be the exemplary model for those who in the twentieth century are endeavoring to reconcile man and nature."

I suspect that in the ur-myth at the source of the Grail legend a figure very much like Merlin held a strong position indeed. Let some naive fool like Perceval or noble knight like Galahad *find* the Grail; it is Merlin – the shaman, the sage, the doctor, the wizard, the poet, the medicine man, the magic man – who knows what to *do* with it. He knows how to prepare and employ it properly. He knows the promise and the dangers of its power. Yet he is but one in a long line of shamans who learned the uses of nature's hallucinogens.

SHAMANISM AND HALLUCINOGENS

Until the 1970s the importance of hallucinogens in shamanism was relatively little known, or at least downplayed. Researchers tended to ignore drug use by shamans or briefly gloss over it. Even Eliade, in his classic *Shamanism,* dealt lightly with the subject, though he noted the error of this approach late in life. He and most others who wrote about shamanism emphasized other methods "medicine men" employed to induce trance – pounding drums or playing other instruments, chanting, dancing, and so on.

Of course, these other "techniques of ecstasy" were and are essential to almost all shamans. Indeed, in some cultures, shamans rely entirely upon them and shun drug use.

However, more recent studies – from Michael J. Harner's *Hallucinogens and Shamanism* and Peter Furst's *Hallucinogens and Culture* in the 1970s to Piers Vitebsky's *The Shaman*, published in 1995 – have shown the use of mind-altering substances to be a part of shamanism as far back as the vocation can be traced. And, of course, the notion of shamanic drug use was popularized by the works of Carlos Castaneda, though the legitimacy of his accounts has been thrown into question and will not be considered here.

Furst begins his introduction to *Hallucinogens and Culture* by pointing out one of the chief landmarks in the growing realization of drug-plants' importance to shamanism, a 1970 "conversation across the disciplines" between ethnobotanist Richard Evans Schultes and anthropologist Weston La Barre, who had known each other ever since they investigated peyote use by Native Americans in 1936. In 1970 La Barre published a paper in *Economic Botany* titled "Old and New World Narcotics: A Statistical Question and an Ethnological

Reply" that employed many of Schultes' psychoactive-plant findings and put them in an anthropological context.

The "statistical question" was posed by Schultes: Why were the original Americans aware of a great number of mind-altering plants while fewer than a dozen had been widely used in the Old World? La Barre's answer was, to quote Furst's summary:

"(1) that the magicoreligious use of hallucinogenic plants by American Indians represents a survival from a very ancient Paleolithic and Mesolithic shamanistic stratum, and that its linear ancestor is likely to be an archaic form of the shamanistic Eurasiatic fly-agaric cults that survived in Siberia into the present century, and (2) that while profound socioeconomic and religious transformations brought about the eradication of ecstatic shamanism and knowledge of intoxicating mushrooms and other plants over most of Eurasia, a very different set of historical and cultural circumstances favored their survival and elaboration in the New World."

The early 1970s also brought a growing acceptance of the fact that humans have experienced a need for drug-induced mind alteration for as long as they have existed. Dr. Andrew T. Weil, long before he became a widely popular figure in the 1990s as a proponent of healthy nutrition and natural remedies, was among those who recognized this need. He wrote in his 1972 book *The Natural Mind* that "the desire to alter consciousness periodically is an innate, normal drive analogous to hunger or the sex drive."

This view would eventually receive its most convincing argument in Ronald K. Siegel's comprehensive book, *Intoxication*. "History shows that we have always used drugs," Siegel wrote in his foreword. "In every age, in every part of this planet, people have pursued intoxication with plant drugs, alcohol, and other mind-altering substances. Surprisingly, we're not the only ones to do this. Almost every species of animal has engaged in the natural pursuit of intoxicants. This behavior has so much force and persistence that it functions like a drive, just like our drives of hunger, thirst, and sex. This 'fourth drive' is a natural part of our biology, creating the irrepressible demand for drugs. In a sense, the war on drugs is a war against ourselves, a denial of our very nature."

HARNER'S *HALLUCINOGENS AND SHAMANISM*

One of the chief proofs of how ancient and integral drug use has been in human history is the importance of intoxicants in "primitive" societies. A groundbreaking work in the understanding of this factor was anthropology professor Michael J. Harner's *Hallucinogens and Shamanism*, first published by Oxford University Press in 1973, nine years before his better-known *Way of the Shaman*. This earlier book was a collection of essays – three by himself, others by such scientists and scholars as Kenneth M. Kensinger ("Banisteriopsis Usage Among the Peruvian Cashinahua"), Janet Siskind ("Visions and Cures Among the Sharanahua"), Henry Munn ("The Mushrooms of Language") and Claudio Naranjo ("Psychological Aspects of the Yage Experience in an Experimental Setting").

In his introduction to the book Harner challenged the preceding scholarly neglect of the role of drugs in shamanism. Central to the shaman's work, he stated, was "the change into another state of consciousness, often called a trance, with the shaman feeling that he is taking a journey." While noting that the "use of psychedelic agents is only one of the ways of achieving the trance-like states conducive to a sense of seeing and contacting the supernatural," Harner said modern research had made it clear that shamans the world over had discovered that "the use of hallucinogens appears to be the easiest and fastest technique for reaching a believed supernatural experience and visions."

He focused on the evidence gathered by Siberian explorers. "Any discussion of hallucinogens and shamanism must consider the relationship between the two in northeast Asia – the home of what has been commonly termed 'classic' shamanism, i.e., as practiced by the native Siberians and the first to be described in detail in the ethnological literature. In this region we find a close relationship between the psychoactive mushroom, fly-agaric (*Amanita muscaria*) and the shamanisitic act."

Nevertheless, protested Harner, the "theoretical literature has largely overlooked the fact that even this 'classic' shamanism often involved the use of [a] hallucinogen."

FURST'S *HALLUCINOGENS AND CULTURE*

Though covering shamanic drug use in various cultures (including Harner's own "The Role of Hallucinogenic Plants in European Witchcraft"), *Hallucinogens and Shamanism* chiefly focused on South American tribes. Understanding of the subject was considerably widened and enriched three years later by Furst's *Hallucinogens and Culture*. A professor of anthropology at the State University of New York at Albany and a research associate at the Botanical Museum of Harvard at the time, Furst laid out a comprehensive and lucid overview that gained praise from Weston La Barre, Andrew Weil, and others.

Furst documented human employment of several drug-plants throughout the Americas, Asia, Africa, Europe and elsewhere. He showed that shamans through the ages have used whatever substance was most effective in their culture at inducing trance – including tobacco, cannabis, *Iboga, Yaje, Ololiuhqui* (morning glory), peyote and mushrooms. In addition, he devoted an entire chapter to "R. Gordon Wasson and the Identification of the Divine *Soma*" as *Amanita muscaria*. Furst's carefully argued and documented book supports his conclusion that "often, though not always or everywhere, the shaman's ecstatic dream has involved the use of some sacred hallucinogenic plant believed to contain a supernatural transforming power over and above the life force or 'soul stuff' that in animistic-shamanistic religious systems inhabits all natural phenomenon..."

VITEBSKY'S *THE SHAMAN*

The role of drug use by shamans as indicated by Schultes, La Barre, Harner and Furst has become generally accepted in more recent surveys of the subject such as Piers Vitebsky's 1995 book, *The Shaman*. In that concise yet edifying study, Vitebsky states: "Hallucinogenic plants show beyond doubt that there can be a physiological basis for shamanic states of consciousness. Yet as with drumming and dancing (or fasting or deprivation of sleep), the cause itself does not explain the content and emotional tone of the shamanic states...

"To shamans," Vitebsky continues, "the plants are actually spirit teachers and by ingesting them the shamans take the spirits' properties into themselves. What the plants reveal is not a deviation from reality but a true reality that in an ordinary state of consciousness remains hidden... The drug-revealed reality is a shared, social reality. Drug taking is not part of an alienated rejection of society, as it so often can be, but a means to a fuller integration of the individual with others...

Vitebsky illustrates this section of his book, "Shamanic Botany: Hallucinogens," with, among other things, a photograph of an *Amanita muscaria*.

AM is the psychedelic sacrament of the ur-shamans of central and northern Asia. As some of the tribes of this area migrated east to Europe, they continued to use and revere the mushroom in a similar fashion until Roman and Christian conquerors persecuted their religious practices and compressed knowledge of the fly agaric's power and role into near-extinction. As other AM-employing people moved south into India, the mushroom became increasingly difficult to find and transport from the nearest point where it grew in profusion, the foothills of the Himalayas. And those who knew the true identity of this "Soma" became fewer and fewer until there were none left who knew the truth behind the *Rig-Veda* passages about it.

What of the Asians who migrated west across the once-existing Aleutian ice bridge to the Americas? They found bountiful specimens of AM, but this American variety, even though it looked exactly the same as the Asian, was just different enough chemically – for reasons that have yet to be determined by scientists – to prove far less useful. As we can easily see by contrasting the experiences of persons who've ingested the North American AM with those of partakers of the Asian variety, the former is far less predictable and satisfactory in its hallucinogenic properties. Consequently, early Native Americans sought out substitute sacraments – and found them in peyote and several other plants.

Meanwhile, Northern Europeans had no such strong stand-ins for the suppressed AM. Could the loss of knowledge about this "magic mushroom" lie behind the legend of the Holy Grail? In our investigation of that legend's mystery, it's time for a close look at the prime suspect.

PART FOUR:
THE PRIME SUSPECT

AM: A TOADSTOOL'S CASE FILE

Perhaps you have been fortunate enough to walk through a forest and encounter the extraordinary sight of *Amanita muscaria* raising its distinctive red-and-white head. Even if you haven't, you surely still must have seen AM many times during your life. The fabulous fungus is a favorite subject of artists who illustrate fairy tales and other children's stories and books, and it adorns the cover of many mushroom guides.

Such popularity is easy to understand. This member of the *Amanita* group (which also contains the world's most dreaded poisonous species, the sickly-white "Death Cap" *Amanita phalloides*) is the most visually striking of the relatively common mushrooms. Frequently called the fly agaric, because of the centuries-old belief that it kills flies (actually, flies that land on chopped-up portions are only temporarily stunned, at best), AM is the classic "toadstool."

Most other mushrooms don't bring such attention to themselves. While there are many other spectacular species, most rise only an inch or two from the ground (or a tree stump, or wherever else they grow) and clothe themselves in modest dull-white, brown or gray. The fly agaric shuns such modesty. Even among its bold cousins of the *Amanita* class, AM is a flamboyant king.

FROM AN EGG TO A TOWER

Like the ugly duckling, *Amanita muscaria* takes a while to show its glory. It starts off very unassuming, the small, round white volva looking like a golf ball or a chicken egg. This grows to a couple of inches in diameter. Then, again like an egg, it breaks open as the cap and stem inside push their way through the top. As the fire-engine-red (or sometimes brilliant orange) cap rises, remnants of the broken volva stick to it, unless washed off by a strong downpour. These broken pieces form an abstract pattern of white patches on the ruddy dome that resemble clouds or scales (and are usually called the latter by mycologists).

The cap is at first bulbous, its bottom circling and clinging to the white stem for a couple of days. It then breaks free from the stem and eventually flattens as it grows even larger, revealing the white, crowded, free gills beneath. A diameter averaging 3½ to 4½ inches is eventually attained. The detachment leaves behind a fringed skirt of white material around the upper part of the stem, commonly called the ring. The bottom of the stem is bulbous and often surrounded – again, if a heavy rain has not washed it away – by the lower remnants of the broken volva, sometimes called the cup.

The overall appearance of these features presents one of nature's most startling spectacles. Though there are several other distinctively colored and shaped fungi, most of AM's neighboring mushrooms are comparatively dull and hidden. Why does nature make the fly agaric so easy to spot?

The mushroom's mind-altering powers might have something to do with it. It is as if AM is calling out to passersby.

Those mind-altering powers, which can be as spectacular as AM's appearance, have made AM a possible influence on a famous book of the 19th Century and landed the toadstool a definite role in novels by two of the 20th Century's most noted writers of American fiction.

AM'S LITERARY ROLES

Two scenes involving mushrooms in Lewis Carroll's classic *Alice in Wonderland* are particularly memorable. In one, the lost girl encounters a giant caterpillar smoking a hookah while reclining on the top of a giant mushroom. In the other, she suddenly grows to huge proportions after eating one side of a mushroom, and shrinks after consuming the other side.

Several writers have proposed that the author – a don at Christ Church College, Oxford, whose real name was Charles Lutwidge Dodgson – was inspired to write this scene after reading an article by British mycologist Mordecai Cooke on the psychoactive effects of *Amanita muscaria,* which appeared in a magazine that Carroll was known to have owned. It has also been suggested that Carroll might have been familiar with one or both of Cooke's books *The Seven Sisters of Sleep: Popular History of the Seven Prevailing Narcotics of the World* (1860) and *A Plain and Easy Account of British Fungi* (1862). Richard Rudgley, in his *The Encyclopedia of Psychoactive Substances* (1998), believes the former "would have had a peculiar resonance for Dodgson, who had seven sisters himself..."

In all three of these sources, Cooke describes how one of AM's effects is the way it makes objects seem larger or smaller than they really are (macroscopia and microscopia).

Rudgley also adds that in a 1996 article titled "Wonderland Revisited" Michael Carmichael "has suggested that this was not just a literary influence but one that encouraged Dodgson to experiment with the mushroom itself. In a meticulous study of the various medical books in Dodgson's personal library Carmichael shows that he would have been aware of the effects and properties of numerous psychoactive substances. There are also numerous veiled references to drug-induced altered states of consciousness in Dodgson's writings."

CHAYEFSKY'S *ALTERED STATES*

Best known for incisive television plays of the 1950s and 60s like *Marty* and later screenplays for powerful films such as *Network* and *Hospital*, Paddy Chayefsky finally got around to writing a novel in the 1970s – one whose subject matter was quite a departure from his previous concerns.

Altered States, published in 1978, tells the story of a young scientist's experiments with drugs and isolation tanks in an effort to determine the origins of consciousness.

The book was obviously based on the experiences of the radical scientist John Lilly. However, while Lilly's emersions were made under the influence of a psychedelic he identified only as "K" (which others have since determined to be ketamine), Chayefsky's Edward Jessup uses a mixture of *Amanita muscaria* and other hallucinatory substances, mainly "white, tuberous roots [that] were sinicuiche or heimia salicifolia."

In the absorbing first half of the 1980 movie version (largely written by Chayefsky but eventually disowned because it deteriorates into horror-film clichés), director Ken Russell has a field day with mushroom symbolism – the protagonist's mind-states involve AM-like umbrellas and a panoply of other hyper-colorful images. *Amanita muscaria* is also named in the film as the mushroom Jessup uses, though we never see a clear visual representation of it.

PYNCHON'S *GRAVITY'S RAINBOW*

AM also pops up in Thomas Pynchon's most lauded and challenging work, the labyrinthine novel *Gravity's Rainbow*.

Pynchon is notoriously elusive, an author who has hidden himself away from the stare of the world even more successfully than J.D. Salinger. However, several years ago I met someone who knew him for a while back in the 1960s, his one-time friend, Joel Siegel – whose own writing has ranged from solid rock-music journalism to extraordinarily unorthodox fiction. Siegel told me that both he and Pynchon have consumed AM, among other psychedelics. That won't surprise many readers of Pynchon, whose unbridled prose, especially in *Gravity's Rainbow*, has the dizzying, vivid swirl of a drug trip.

On page 105 of *Gravity's Rainbow* (Bantam paperback version) a female character is "alone in the house, except for the secret cameraman and Osbie Feel, who's out in the kitchen, doing something mysterious with a harvest of mushrooms from up on the roof. They have shiny red-orange cups [sic – this may have been a typo where "caps" was meant] with raised patches of whitish-gray veil. Now and then the geometry of her restlessness brings her to glace [sic] in a doorway at his boyish fussing with the *Amanita muscaria* (for it is this peculiar relative of the poisonous Destroying Angel that claims Osbie's attention, or what passes with him for attention)..." The "Destroying Angel" is the deadly *Amanita phalloides*.

"What can young Osbie possibly have in mind? He is carefully scraping out the inside of each persimmon-colored mushroom cup [sic] and shredding the rest. Dispossessed elves run around up on the roof, gibbering. He now has a growing heap of orange-gray fungus, which he proceeds to add in fistfuls to a pot of steaming water. A previous batch also simmers atop the stove, reduced to a thick gruel covered with yellow scum, which Osbie now and then purees further in Pirate's blending machine. Then he spreads the fungoid mush over a tin cookie sheet. He opens the oven, removes with asbestos potholders another sheet covered with dark caked dust, and replaces it with the one has just prepared. With a mortar and pestle he pulverizes the substance and dumps it into an old Huntley & Palmers biscuit tin, reserving only enough to roll deftly up in a Rizla liquorice cigarette paper, light, and inhale the smoke of."

In *Gravity's Rainbow* it is as difficult to distinguish fantasy (or at least otherworldliness) from reality as it is to separate the typos from Pynchon's possibly peculiar word choice. Did he really write "cup" for "cap"? And can AM really be potent in this cigarette form? Perhaps, though I've never come across any other mention of it.

However, one aspect of this passage does seem to be pure poetic license: Unlike *psilocybe* and some other varieties of mushroom, *Amanita muscaria* cannot yet be cultured. It must be found in the wild, growing beneath one of its associate trees.

That is, unless Pynchon knows something the rest of us don't. And I wouldn't put it past him.

TOM ROBBINS' 'SUPERFLY'

Another noted modern novelist, Tom Robbins, has also written about *Amanita muscaria*.

Robbins, who lives in a small town on Washington's rain-forest Olympia peninsula, writes novels that are, in their own way, as unconventional as Pynchon's. They follow their own logic down dream-like paths that either delight or exasperate readers.

However, an article written for the December 1976 issue of the drug-oriented magazine *High Times* proves that Robbins is capable of fairly standard, informative, if characteristically lively prose. The piece, "Superfly: The Toadstool That Conquered the Universe," is still the most readable introduction to AM that I've encountered, and I'll quote passages from it later in the portion of this chapter describing the fly agaric's ingestion and effects.

First, though, a little history....

FIRST EUROPEAN REPORTS ON AM USE IN SIBERIA

Amanita muscaria has been ingested for its psychedelic properties ever since one of our braver ancestors decided to give it a nibble untold centuries ago. However, even though there is a record of its use by tribes ranging from North America to the Balkans, and medieval Europeans mixed chopped AM with milk to kill (or at least stun) flies – thus the name, *muscaria* being Latin for "fly-catching" – documentation of the mushroom's effects on humans came only after

European travelers and prisoners began reporting on AM use by Siberian peoples.

The earliest detailed account came from a Swedish army officer named Philip John von Strahlenberg, who had been incarcerated in a Siberian prison. He wrote in 1730 that members of the Ostyak and Vogul tribes told him that they preferred the inebriation gained from ingesting AM to the effects of Russian vodka. However, the most interesting descriptions of Siberian AM use came from a German naturalist, Georg Heinrich von Langsdorf, in 1809, and a Swedish-American ethnologist Waldemar Jochelson in 1905 and 1908.

In his *Soma: Divine Mushroom of Immortality*, probably the most valuable book ever written about *Amanita muscaria* (which deserves, and will get, its own chapter), R. Gordon Wasson offered 125 pages of excerpts from scientific and other AM accounts and studies, including Langsdorf's and Jochelson's reports.

THE NATURE OF THE ECSTASY

Langsdorf, in Wasson's excerpt, wrote of finding that "fly-agarics grow almost everywhere in Kamchatka," the huge peninsula at the far eastern end of what was then Russia and would soon become the Soviet Union. Among the members of two tribes there, the Kamchadals and the Koryaks, the usual way of consuming the mushrooms was "to dry them and then to swallow them at one gulp, rolled up into a ball, without chewing them; chewing fly-agarics is considered harmful, since it is said to cause digestive disturbances." However, sometimes "these mushrooms are cooked fresh and eaten in soups or sauces, since they then taste more like the usual edible mushrooms and have a weaker effect... Occasionally, too, fly-agarics are soaked in berry juice, which one may thereafter drink at his pleasure as a genuine intoxicating wine..."

AM's effect "begins to manifest itself about a half hour after eating, in a pulling or jerking of the muscles..." This is followed by "a sense of things swimming before the eyes, dizziness, and sleep." Overindulgence sometimes causes vomiting. "The nature of the ecstasy or drunkenness caused by the fly-agaric resembles the effects of wine or vodka to the extent that it renders unconscious the persons intoxicated with it and arouses in them feelings that are mostly joyful, less often gloomy. The face becomes red, bloated, and

... the intoxicated person begins to do and say many things involuntarily." Sometimes the inebriated ones "appear to be dancing and making the most outlandish pantomime movements with their hands... According to their own statement, persons who are slightly intoxicated feel extraordinarily light on their feet and are then exceedingly skillful in bodily movements and physical exercise."

Langsdorf next notes the acuteness of vision and the distortion of distances and the size of objects often associated with AM consumption: "[I]f one wishes to step over a small stick or a straw, he steps and jumps as though the obstacles were tree trunks." AM also appears to have worked as some sort of "truth drug" on the Siberian partakers: a man "voluntarily blurts out secrets, fully conscious of his actions and aware of his secret but unable to hold his nerves in check." In this condition a man who is fond of dancing dances and a music-lover sings incessantly. Others run or walk quite involuntarily, "without any intention of moving, to places where they do not wish to go at all."

Some partakers experience a real or imagined sense of greater bodily strength: "[T]hese persons exert muscular efforts of which they would be completely incapable at other times; for example, they have carried heavy burdens with the greatest of ease, and eye-witnesses have confirmed to me the fact that a person in a state of fly-agaric ecstasy carried a 120-pound sack of flour a distance of 10 miles, although at any other time he would scarcely have been able to lift a load easily."

GOING TO EXTREMES FOR ECSTASY

Then Langsdorf describes the part of Siberian AM ingestion that has most startled (and often disgusted) Western readers.

"But the strangest and most remarkable feature of the fly-agaric is its effect on the urine. The Koryaks have known since time immemorial that the urine of a person who has consumed fly-agarics has a stronger narcotic and intoxicating power than the fly-agaric itself and that this effect persists for a long time after consumption. For example, a man may be moderately drunk on fly-agarics today and by tomorrow may have completely slept off this moderate intoxication and be sober; but if he now drinks a cup of his own urine, he will become far more intoxicated than ... before."

This feature leads to other practices that may seem even more extreme (and comic) to people of other cultures: “Among the Koryaks ... it is quite common for a sober man to lie in wait for a man intoxicated with mushrooms and, when the latter urinates, to catch the urine secretly in a container and this way to obtain a stimulating drink even though he has no mushrooms.”

One hundred years later, Jochelson recorded the same practices. “There is reason to think that the effect of fly-agaric would be stronger were not its alkaloid quickly taken out of the organism with the urine. The Koryak know this by experience, and the urine of persons intoxicated with fly-agaric is not wasted. The drunkard himself drinks it to prolong his hallucinations, or he offers it to others as a treat.”

THE SINGING SHAMAN

Jochelson also confirmed Langsdorf's observations regarding methods of ingestion and effects: “The Koryak do not eat the fly-agaric fresh. The poison is then more effective, and kills more speedily. The Koryak say that three fresh fungi suffice to kill a person.” [Wasson would later challenge the widespread assumption that AM kills at all, even in heavy doses, despite the fact that it is described as “poison” in almost all mushroom guides.] Accordingly, fly-agaric is dried in the sun or over the hearth after it has been gathered.

“Like certain other vegetable poisons, as opium and hashish, the alkaloid of fly-agaric produces intoxication, hallucinations, and delirium. Light forms of intoxication are accompanied by a certain degree of animation and some spontaneity of movements... Under strong intoxication, the senses become deranged; surrounding objects appear either very large or very small, hallucinations set in, spontaneous movements, and convulsions. So far as I could observe, attacks of great animation alternate with moments of deep depression. The person intoxicated by fly-agaric sits quietly rocking from side to side, even taking part in the conversation with his family. Suddenly his eyes dilate, he begins to gesticulate convulsively, converses with persons whom he imagines he sees, sings and dances. Then an interval of rest sets in again.”

The most important AM-intoxicated singer is the person in one of the tribes that Jochelson investigated – the Kamchadal, the Koryaks and the Chukchee – who combined gifts for music and storytelling in hopes of healing. "Many shamans, previous to their séances," the ethnologist reported, "eat fly-agaric in order to get into ecstatic states."

MODERN ASSESSMENTS OF AM'S EFFECTS

Sixty years after Jochelson's accounts, Wasson – who, by this time, had become the world's most prominent ethnomycologist (a term he had to invent himself to describe someone who studies fungi's effect on human beings) – revised the earlier findings about AM's effects somewhat after studying mushroom use around the world. He said in 1967 that fly agaric "begins to act in fifteen or twenty minutes and the effects last for hours." And the first effect is "soporific. One goes to sleep for about two hours, and the sleep is not normal. One cannot be roused from it, but is sometimes aware of the sounds round about. In this half-sleep sometimes one has colored visions that respond, at least to some extent, to one's desires."

Two decades before he became a best-selling author of books on holistic health, Dr. Andrew Weil specialized in writing on psychedelic substances. In a May 1982 article for *High Times*, he wrote that AM "can transport people quite safely to realms of powerful, nonordinary experience."

Not always pleasant experiences, however.

Unlike Wasson and the Siberian explorers, Weil had largely based his observations on AM use in Northern California, where results were mixed at best. Weil tried to explain this by writing that "*Amanita muscaria* does not kill, but it does make the body feel very unusual. This strong but neutral change may be interpreted in one of two ways: as a negative, outside force operating against the ego – that is, as sickness or intoxication – or as an opportunity to withdraw attention to strange ones – that is, as an altered state of consciousness or high."

That factor – plus the conditions that surround the ingestion of any psychedelic (the physical and mental condition of the taker, his or her attitude, what Timothy Leary termed "set and setting," and so on) – certainly can play a part. However, my own readings about fly agarics and casual conversations with people who have consumed specimens found in California and the Pacific Northwest lead me to believe that there's one big reason for poor results: a crucial difference in the chemical makeup of American (and, possibly, European) AM from the Siberian AM.

A VARIETY OF FLY AGARICS

Even back in the early 19th Century, Langsdorf remarked that "some difference exists between Kamchadal mushrooms and those of our own country: the Kamchadal mushroom has a cap with a navel-like protuberance in the middle, its stalk seems to grow thicker towards the base, and, in particular, the lamellae, or gills, may be yellowish rather than white." And, in more recent times, mycologists have named at least four distinctive variations of *muscaria* – *flavivolvata* (red-orange cap), *regalis* (red-brown cap), *formosa* (yellow-orange cap) and *alba* (whitish cap). These are generally associated with particular growth ranges. For instance, fly agarics found in the Eastern U.S. (chiefly in the New England states) tend to be the *formosa* variety, while those growing along the West Coast are more likely to be *flavivolvata*.

The similar appearance of the red-capped *muscarias* of the Pacific Northwest and those of Asia, however, does not mean they contain the same active ingredients in even approximately equal amounts. Scientific analyses of these components have come up with radically different results over the span of just a few decades. A half-century ago, muscarine (first isolated in *A. muscaria*; thus its name) was thought to be the main cause of the mushroom's actions. However, a University of Washington study in the 1970s proved that the amount of muscarine in AM is so small as to be negligible. The same study, led by Dr. Robert C. Benedict, isolated the rare substances ibotenic acid and muscimole in the mushroom, citing them as probable chief intoxicants, but adding the suspicion that another, even more elusive ingredient might be present.

In any case, what has been known with certainty for some time is that the active substances vary greatly from mushroom to mushroom, let alone from region to region. And Western U.S. fly agarics seem to be among the most unpredictable.

A FAMOUS NOVELIST'S EXPERIENCES

Despite its spotted reputation, the Western North American variety of *Amanita muscaria* does apparently have Siberian-like effects at least some of the time. There are some scattered reports of AM use by Native Americans. And some of the more adventurous participants in the "drug revolution" of the 1960s and 70s made their own experiments with the mushroom.

Probably the most colorful account of such experiences is the one written by noted novelist Tom Robbins in his previously mentioned *High Times* article:

"I have eaten the fly agaric three times. On the second of those occasions I experienced nothing but a slight nausea. The other times I got gloriously, colossally drunk.

"I say 'drunk' rather than 'high' because I was illuminated by none of the sweet oceanic electricity that it has been my privilege to conduct after swallowing mescaline or LSD-25. On acid, I felt that I was an integral component of the universe. On *muscaria* I felt that I *was* the universe. There was no sense of ego loss. Quite the contrary: I was a superhero who could lick any archangel in town and the rusty boxcar it hoboed in on."

In suggesting what he believed to be the safest way to consume AM, Robbins also touched on the unpredictability of the Western U.S. variety's components.

"The smartest plan is to eat small amounts of mushroom (or sip small amounts of the juice) at half-hour intervals, for it is impossible to gauge the dosage... The amount of 'poison' will vary greatly from place to place, season to season, even mushroom to mushroom."

ADDED FINDINGS

Information about Siberian AM use has been more forthcoming since the end of the Cold War. More recent reports about how Siberian tribes and their shamans employ the mushroom are presented in Richard Rudgley's *The Encyclopedia of Psychoactive Substances*.

Rudgley's studies of prehistoric and ancient drug use led to his winning the first British Museum Prometheus Award and also to his first book, *The Alchemy of Culture: Intoxicants in Society*.

Among the more interesting findings in his encyclopedia is that Siberians who partake of AM distinguish between small, younger specimens and larger, more mature ones. However, this distinction is a bit complicated. "They recommend the former should be used for a stimulant effect as required for work tasks involving considerable physical labour, and the latter for experiencing hallucinogenic effects. Yet, in eastern Siberia, the native people warn that the 'big fungi are not so obedient as small ones, they may deceive; small fungi are stronger than the big ones but more submissive.' They also say that it is important to tell the mushroom (either out loud or to oneself) what you want from it, otherwise it may lead you astray."

Some Siberians prefer to take the mushroom before going to sleep and experience its effects in their dreams.

In "three provisos" meant to "ensure that the altered states of consciousness they experienced were positive ones" – somewhat akin to Timothy Leary's cautions about "set and setting" for LSD use – some Siberians recommend: "First, if an individual was deemed weak then they were given only an extract from the mushroom. Second, they made sure that the user was not interfered with during such altered states in order to avoid both a 'bad trip' and any chance that the user might accidentally injure themselves [sic] or come to any other harm. Finally, the mushroom was not taken with alcohol as the two were seen to be highly incompatible."

Some Siberian societies, such as the Kets and the Forest Nenets, restricted AM use to shamans.

Petrographs (rock carvings) discovered by N.N. Dikov at Pegtymel in Chukotka in the mid-1960s that depict men and women with mushroom-shaped heads, or with mushrooms balanced on their heads or floating just above them (illustrated on page 103 of the *Encyclopedia*) demonstrate, in Rudgley's view, "the antiquity of the eastern Siberian use of the fly-agaric."

"Czelkutq and the Amanita Girls," a Kamchadal folk tale collected by Jochelson that tells of a man who runs away with fairy folk to indulge in the pleasures of the mushroom, as well as traditions of small people seen under the influence of AM in Kamchadal, Koryak and Chukchi societies, indicate "strong links between a belief in 'the little people' and the use of psychoactive substances." (Could the same links be made between Irish beliefs in "little people" and AM use?)

In Siberia, "violent behavior is almost completely unheard of in relation to fly-agaric use," he adds.

THE ANCIENT ONE

As Robbins indicated in his *High Times* article, AM is not superior to certain other psychedelics in providing transcendentally mind-altering experiences, and perhaps is not even their equal. However, what does set the fly agaric apart from such other substances (natural or synthesized) as LSD and mescaline is this: Human beings have used it far longer.

Two factors back up this assertion.

First, AM is easily the most widespread psychedelic. In contrast to the far-more-limited ranges of others such as the psilocybe mushroom and the peyote cactus, AM appears throughout huge portions of North America, Europe and Asia.

Secondly, there's fly agaric's unique appearance. Unlike the peyote cactus, the marijuana plant, the relatively lowly and indistinct psilocybe, or any other natural source of inebriation, AM does not blend into nature's panoply. It is not green or any other common color. It raises its fiery-red, white-spotted head and practically shouts out for attention. It is almost irresistibly inviting and intriguing.

Surely, adventurous prehistoric men and women would have sampled it thousands of years before getting around to less likely candidates for intoxication.

And when those pharmacological pioneers first bit into one of these alluring sprouts, what new visions and ideas would have resulted? Many modern researchers and writers believe that this early consumption of AM profoundly shaped concepts of humanity's relationship to nature, deity and the cosmos – concepts that evolved into traditions that continue to this day.

The earliest still-enduring manifestation is Soma, the priest-exhilarating god/plant of the *Rig-Veda*, the oldest text of not only Hinduism but of all the world's religions.

THE SOMA SOLUTION: A BANKER'S 'DIVINE MUSHROOM'

Sometime between 5,000 and 8,000 years ago, a huge expanse of land – stretching from modern Iran to central India and centered on the fertile valley of the Indus – was overrun and subdued by a people from the north who called themselves Aryans. These chariot-riding, nomadic warriors and their families brought with them a rich culture. They grew grain, bred animals, spoke and wrote the earliest form of Indo-European (upon which Sanskrit, Latin, German, English and many of the future world's languages would be based). They also brought with them a religious mythology teeming with rituals, sacrifices and a pantheon of gods.

One of these gods, Soma, was unique – not only in the Aryan tradition, but in all subsequent faiths.

Soma was not your everyday, cloud-hidden deity. It had descended from the heavens, but then grew out of the earth. It was something that could be gathered by people, and it was something that they could, after ritually rendering it into a juice, consume. It had strong effects upon those who did so. However (unlike what a Christian might experience after partaking of the communion wafer and wine) its effects were not merely symbolic. The consumer of Soma experienced holiness directly, taking on – or at least it seemed – the power to move anything, even the earth itself, and to fly from this world into the realms of heaven.

Over the last two centuries, Vedic scholars have attempted to identify Soma. Hundreds of plants – including *Cannabis indica, Ephedra vulgaris* and even such much more mundane candidates as rhubarb – were suggested. But they simply wouldn't do.

After all, the *Rig-Veda* (also spelled as *Rigveda* and *RgVeda*), the oldest of Hinduism's four Vedas, composed circa 1200 B.C., describes Soma as having no leaves, no seed, no root, no flower and no fruit. Its color was not green, but red or gold.

Aryan priests gathered Soma in the mountains, where it had been planted by an eagle that had transported it from the heavens. Using stones, the priests pressed out the juice of Soma into wooden bowls, then filtered the extract through layers of wool, mixing in some clarified butter. The resulting liquid (no fermentation is mentioned, and, in any case, the effects hardly seem those of mere alcohol) was employed in several rites. In the fire ritual, the Agnistoma, the juice was poured over a fire. The smoke rose to the heavens, where it emboldened the gods – notably Indra – to fight cosmic battles against demons and other enemies of the Aryan community.

After treating the gods, the priests themselves imbibed Soma. And since they were, in the shamanic tradition, also their people's poets, they composed verses in praise of the god/plant, exalting its extraordinary effects:

"I in my grandeur have surpassed the sky and this vast earth. I am great! Great! Flying to the skies! Have I not drunk the Soma?" (*Rig-Veda* 10.119.8, 12).

"The splendid drops I have sipped have set me free." (*Rig-Veda* 8.48.3, 5).

The man that looked at this evidence and came up with the most accepted explanation for the true identity of Soma had no official grounding in Vedic literature or botany. He came from, of all places, American banking.

FROM MONEY TO MUSHROOMS

Robert Gordon Wasson [1898-1986], born in Montana, grew up in Newark, New Jersey. A banker by profession, Wasson climbed the corporate ladder to become vice president of J.P. Morgan & Co. Working with his wife, Valentina, Wasson also gained recognition as an ethnobotanist specializing in the role of hallucinatory mushrooms in the history of culture.

In 1955 Wasson became the first white in recorded history to eat 'sacred mushrooms,' which were administered to him by Maria Sabina, the renowned Oaxacan witch. His are probably the most poetically moving and philosophically convincing accounts of drug-induced experiences ever published. Mushrooms, Russia and History *(1957) was the first of several books by Wasson that traced the origins of many world religions to psychedelic mushroom or lysergic acid cults.*

Timothy Leary,
in one of the biographical sketches that opens
each chapter of his autobiography, *Flashbacks*

Robert Gordon Wasson was born in Great Falls, Montana, on September 22, 1898, and grew up, as Leary notes, in Newark, New Jersey. The Episcopalian clergyman's son spent his sixteenth year studying and traveling in France and Spain. He returned to attend Columbia University, but in 1917 he enlisted in the U.S. Army and served 14 months as a radio operator for the American Expeditionary Force.

After the war, he earned a Bachelor's degree in Literature from Columbia and was the first to be granted a Pulitzer Traveling Scholarship. He studied in London and traveled through Europe. Back in America in 1921, he taught English at Columbia, where one of his students was poet Langston Hughes. Wasson then concentrated on a career in journalism. By 1925 he was writing a daily column, primarily about Wall Street, for the financial pages of the *Herald Tribune*.

Between 1926 and 1928 Wasson's life was marked by three important events. He married the Russian-born pediatrician Valentina Pavlovna. He left financial journalism to take a position with the Guaranty Company of New York (he'd move over to J.P. Morgan & Company in 1934 and became a vice president in 1943). And he discovered mushrooms.

This last event occurred when the Wassons were enjoying a delayed honeymoon in the Catskills. As the couple strolled along a country lane, Valentina suddenly broke away and ran into a meadow. She'd spied a group of mushrooms, and knelt before them with a delight that shocked her new husband. His shock turned to disgust as she began to gather the mushrooms and carried them back to him, saying she would prepare them for their dinner that night.

Gordon, with the typical American distrust of any mushrooms other than those found on a grocery shelf, thought his wife had gone slightly mad, and he refused to have anything to do with her find.

However, his curiosity became aroused when Valentina informed him that hunting wild mushrooms was a common pastime in her native Russia, where most rural people were taught in childhood how to distinguish some of the more common edible species. He soon began to read up on mushrooms. His view of them as "repugnant fungal growths, manifestations of parasitism and decay" transformed completely into "a visceral urge, a love for mushrooms that passeth all understanding."

This new interest grew into an obsession – one that Valentina shared.

During the next 30 years the Wassons spent as much of their spare time as possible learning about these mysterious sprouts of nature, studying the etymology and folklore connected with them. The couple was particularly fascinated with sharply varying attitudes toward mushrooms: the intriguing schism between "mycophilic" (mushroom-loving) areas of the world – the Slavic countries and southern France, as well as parts of Germany, Italy, Austria, Spain and many still-primitive regions – and the "mycophobic" (mushroom-fearing) ones, most of the remaining world.

As Jay Stevens writes in his history of psychedelic drugs in the United States, *Storming Heaven: LSD and the American Dream*:

"Gradually a thesis emerged. The Wassons began to suspect that a mushroom had played a formative role in the ur-religion of tribal Indo-Europe. Their prime candidate was the fly amanite [*Amanita muscaria*], considered by mycophobes to be the most poisonous mushroom of all, although there was no solid evidence that anyone had ever died from eating a fly amanite. What did occur was a species of delirium that, to quote from Cooke's *Plain and Easy Account of British Fungi* (1862), caused one to 'prophesy wildly, engage in feats of prodigious physical exertions, and enjoy illusions of miraculous mobility and metamorphosis.'"

THE FLESH OF THE GODS

In 1957 the Wassons published their massive, privately printed work *Mushrooms, Russia and History* in a limited edition of 500 copies. The book received little notice. However, during the same year millions of Americans learned the name of R. Gordon Wasson when *Life* magazine devoted a 15-page spread to his Mexican mushroom expeditions.

The article, "Great Adventures III: The Discovery of Mushrooms That Cause Strange Visions," appeared in the May 13, 1957 issue of *Life*. The text consisted of Wasson's own description of what it was like to be "bemushroomed," as he put it, and the story was accompanied by more than 20 photographs and sketches.

Despite the article's title, Wasson wasn't the first "discoverer" of the medicinal/religious use of mind-altering mushrooms by Oaxacan natives. Others had bucked the prevailing scientific skepticism at old Spanish accounts of Native Americans using mushrooms in this way – the Aztecs called them *teonanacatl*, "flesh of the gods." Most important was Austrian-born physician and amateur botanist Dr. Blas Pablo Reko, who insisted in the 1930s that the mushrooms were still in use. Seeking to prove it, he was joined on a trip to Oaxaca in 1938 by ethnobotanist Richard Evans Schultes, who wrote a seminal paper on their findings in 1941.

One of the scientists who accompanied Wasson in *his* first journey to Oaxaca in 1953 (along with leading French mycologist Roger Heim) was Austrian-born Mexican ethnologist Roberto J. Weitlander, who had, with son-in-law Jean Bassett Johnson, observed mushroom ceremonies in 1938.

However, in 1955, on the third of his annual journeys to Oaxaca, Wasson and some of his companions became the first outsiders to take part in a mushroom ceremony. On that and subsequent visits, he and his entourage, including Valentina and photographer Allan B. Richardson, first documented in detail the *veladas*, the night-long mushroom-ingesting rites. Wasson's other major contribution was his bringing in scientists like Heim and, later, LSD synthesist Albert Hofmann, who took back species of *psilocybe* to Europe and eventually determined the mushrooms' chemical components.

Wasson's interest in the Mexican mushroom ceremonies had been awakened three years earlier, when Robert Graves (the famed poet and author of the popular historical novel *I, Claudius*) sent him Schultes' 1941 article. Wasson telephoned Schultes, who offered encouragement and information, and the next year Gordon and Valentina undertook the first of their several visits to the Mazatec Indians of central Mexico. There he won the immeasurably helpful cooperation of a village *curandera* (spiritual healer), Maria Sabina, who conducted the shamanic rites.

In the preface to *The Sacred Mushroom Seeker*, a collection of essays about Wasson, editor Thomas J. Riedlinger notes: "Many contend his *Life* article launched, or at least helped trigger, the 'psychedelic revolution' of the 1960s. (Timothy Leary, for example, was influenced by it to eat magic mushrooms in Mexico before trying LSD or any other hallucinogen.) Gordon deplored this development because he felt the mushrooms were being used casually, for recreation, rather than respectfully for spiritual enlightenment."

Though Leary wrote in his book *High Priest* that he regarded Wasson as his spiritual guide, Gordon almost always disparaged the Harvard lecturer, telling Riedlinger in 1985: "He's vain and superficial... reckless. There's no scholarship there."

Leary generally took Wasson's attitude toward him is his usual, good-natured stride. But others were offended. One of the most prolific writers about psychedelics, Andrew Weil, who would become a best-selling author of holistic health books in the 1990s, wrote in the October-December 1988 edition of *The Journal of Psychoactive Drugs*:

"Wasson was a snob and an elitist about psychedelics, relegating most of those who have experimented with sacred substances to the category of 'the Tim Learys and their ilk.' Who is he to judge whether others' uses of psychedelics are or are not religious? ... Wasson was partly responsible for bringing knowledge of sacramental plants and molecules to the masses, yet he was never comfortable with his role as a popularizer and founder of the psychedelic movement. Perhaps the elitist tone of his writing was rooted in that discomfort."

Paradoxically, perhaps, Wasson opposed laws banning use of hallucinogens, even going so far as to write: "If I had my way, I would make the psychoactive drugs (except alcoholic beverages) as cheap as possible. I would make them available in every drug store without prescription to anyone."

In any case, following Wasson's *Life* article and the work of those it influenced (not just Leary but Carlos Castaneda and many others) the lowly *psilocybe* mushroom quickly rose from obscurity to become – with marijuana, LSD and mescaline (peyote) – one of the four most-used and most-discussed psychedelic drugs of the 1960s and afterward.

And, as Peter Furst wrote in *Hallucinogens and Culture*: "In a very real sense, Gordon's 1955 experience with the sacred mushrooms changed his life. For, having spent most of his professional career on Wall Street, he went on to devote the next 30 years not just to library research on mushrooms, his favorite subject, but also to numerous field trips and painstaking ethnobotanical and ethnohistorical studies of the several species of sacred mushrooms and other divinatory plants still in use among some Mexican Indians."

In 1963, four years after the death of his wife, Wasson shifted his attention to the opposite side of the world. And this time he solved a mystery that others had been trying to unravel for centuries.

IDENTIFYING SOMA

Throughout the two centuries after Sanskrit was initially translated into English and other European languages, scholars attempted to solve the greatest mystery of the Vedas, which can be stated in two questions: Was Soma a real, earthly substance? If so, what substance was it?

All sorts of possibilities were presented, among them *Ephedra vulgaris, Cannibis indica, Ipomoea muricata, Sarcostemma brevistigma* and various species of *Euphorbia*. However, as anthropologist Weston La Barre noted, none of these proposed plants "has carried any conviction, and all are implausible philologically, botanically, and pharmacodynamically. It is no wonder that most ranking twentieth-century scholars have come to regard the problem of Soma as insoluble."

That is, until Wasson came along.

Understanding Wasson's Soma theory – how a psychoactive substance can be poeticized into a holy sacrament – will make it much easier to comprehend my own theory, which proposes that the same "magic mushroom" became romanticized into the legend of the Holy Grail. And though he and I have little else in common, we both come to our mushroom and our theories as "mere amateurs."

Eminent religious historian Huston Smith had some cogent things to say about Wasson's unorthodox standing in "Historical Evidence: India's Sacred Soma," one of the essays collected in his definitive study of the relationship between drugs and religion, *Cleansing the Doors of Perception*:

"[T]he longer one ponders the Soma discovery, the more facets of Gordon Wasson appear relevant until one has to remind oneself that it wasn't the preordained purpose for which he was born... [T]he careers Wasson pursued on his way to Soma were only seeming detours. English and journalism gave him a feel for language which was to grace his report when it appeared, and banking, being lucrative, enabled him to travel when fieldwork beckoned and to consult the authorities whose diverse areas of expertise – Sanskrit, history, philology, comparative mythology, folklore, art, poetry, literature, ecology, ethnobotany, phytochemistry, and pharmacology – he was to fit with his own mycological knowledge to craft the solution...

"Finally, it was in Wasson's favor that he was not an academic.... The problem called for an amateur, a man who could approach it with innocence and love and across disciplinary boundaries."

Wasson's 381-page *Soma: Divine Mushroom of Immortality* was first published by Harcourt/Brace in a limited hardbound edition in 1968 and then as a trade paperback in 1973. It included a post-Vedic history of the god/plant by Sanskrit scholar Wendy Doniger O'Flaherty and ended with a 125-page section of "Exhibits" – chiefly devoted to excerpts from reports on the fly agaric in Siberia by explorers, travelers, anthropologists, linguists and others.

Between these two bookends Wasson laid out his theory about Soma's identity. His main points were the following:

The *Rig-Veda* does not refer to "the root of the Soma plant, nor to its leaves, nor to its blossoms, nor to its seed." Either there "must have been a conspiracy of silence, laid down perhaps by the dictates of their very religion," or the Vedic poets were truly speaking of a plant that had none of these features – '*viz.*, a mushroom.'"

Soma was gathered in the mountains, probably the Hindu Kush or the Himalayas. Wasson quotes a dozen passages from the *Rig-Veda*, including: "...these Somas grown on the mountain top." (IX 18, 1a); "Born on the mountain top...the Soma juice is placed for Indra." (IX 62, 15a); "This Soma juice, god [himself], sitting on the mountain..." (IX 98, 9c).

Soma was not alcoholic. "The difference in tone between the bibulous verse of the West and holy rapture of the Soma hymns will suffice for those of any literary discrimination or psychological insight... The stalks were pressed as a liturgical act and before the liturgy was finished the juice was drunk... The Indo-Iranians did not know the distillation process and therefore Soma could not have been a strong drink, i.e., brandy or the distillate of grains."

Soma was not *bhang* (the Indian name for *Cannabis sativa*, also known as marijuana, hemp and hashish). "[T]he RgVeda placed Soma only on the high mountains, whereas hemp grows everywhere; and [it stated] that the virtue of Soma lay in the stalks, whereas it is the resin of the unripened pistillate buds of hashish that transport one into the beyond; or, much weaker, the leaves, which are never mentioned in the RgVeda. The stalks of hemp are woody."

Soma is never described as green, black, blue or gray. Its color is most often termed *hari*.

"*Hari* is the precise adjective that one would wish to employ in Vedic to describe the fly-agaric," Wasson asserts. "*Hari* is not only a colour word: the intensity of the colour is also expressed by it. It is dazzling, brilliant, lustrous, resplendent, flaming. In colour it seems to have run from red to light yellow. The mythological horses of the sun-god were *hari*...

"The poets of the RgVeda not only use the same adjective for Soma and the sun-god's horses. They compare Soma directly with the sun. The sun is a shining disc and thus a compelling metaphor for the fly-agaric, as compelling as it is inappropriate for any chlorophyll-bearing plant."

Among the passages referring to Soma's color in the *Rig-Veda,* says Wasson, are these:

"He [Soma] shines together with the sun..." (IX 2, 6c)

"[H]e has clothed himself with the fire-bursts of the sun." (IX 71, 9b)

"He [Soma] wraps himself all around with the rays of the sun." (IX 86, 32a)

Wasson also notes that the *Rig-Veda* often ties Soma to Agni, the god of fire, "to the point where [religious scholar Abel] Bergaigne even went so far as to advance the hypothesis that the two had been interchangeable."

Other passages in the *Rig-Veda* describe Soma in terms that seem to otherwise refer to AM's appearance and manner of growth.

For example, there seems to be a description of AM's brilliantly radiant cap with its white, cloud-like spots or scales at IX 69, 5: "With unfading vesture, brilliant, newly clothed, the immortal *hari wraps himself all around.* By authority he has taken the back of heaven to clothe himself in, a spread-cloth like to a cloud..."

Even more striking is this apparent account (IX 71, 2) of Soma/AM's growth: "Aggressive as a killer of peoples he advances, bellowing with power. He sloughs off the Asurian [referring to the Vedic divinities, the Asuras] colour that is his. He abandons his envelope, goes to the rendezvous with the Father. With what floats he makes continually his vesture-of-grand-occasion." In this passage, Wasson equates envelope with the mushroom's universal veil and "Father" with sky.

Other passages seem to describe Soma/AM symbolically as an animal. For instance:

"Like a serpent he creeps out of his old skin." (IX 86, 44c)

"He [Soma] bellows, [a] terrifying bull, with might, sharpening his shining [*hari*] horns, gazing afar. The Soma rests in his well-appointed birthplace. The hide is of bull, the dress of sheep." (IX 70, 7)

Wasson points out "four poetic conceits" which, he says, symbolize *Amanita muscaria*. These are:

The single eye. "Quickened by the seven minds, he [Soma] has encouraged the rivers free of grief, which have strengthened his single eye." (IX 9, 4) "[Soma] who has for eye the sun." (IX 97, 46c)

Mainstay of the sky. "Thou Soma art the mainstay of the sky...." (IX 109, 6a) "Mainstay of the sky, foundation of the earth, all establishments are in the hand of this [Soma]...." (IX 89, 6ab).

The Navel. Wasson says that this word, *nabhi* in Sanskrit, denotes both an umbilicus and "the 'hub' of a wheel." He points out that "navel" is often used in other societies to refer to a mushroom. "Soma is the Navel of the Way." (IX 74, 4) "The sharp seer, in heaven's navel, is magnified in the woolen filtre, Soma the wise, possessed of good intelligence" (IX 12, 4).

The Filtres. "In the RgVeda," Wasson writes, "filtres figure prominently. One of them, a filtre of lamb's wool, presents no problem.... But the RgVeda speaks of two other filtres that have always baffled the scholars."

The woolen filtre, Wasson says, is actually the middle filtre. The first, "in order of their function," is a celestial filtre, where the sun's rays "spread over the back of heaven, the filtre, O Soma...." (IX 66, 5abc). Wasson concludes that this "back" is the pileus (cap) of the fly agaric. The third filtre is far more vaguely mentioned, but after running through it the "Soma-juice" is "clarified," becoming "Fortune" and "the Giver of the Gift" (IX 97, 55). Wasson believes that this third filtre is purposely obscure because it refers to the human kidney's filtering effect on AM's active elements, and Soma, in its ultimate stage, "issues forth as sparkling yellow urine, retaining its inebriating virtue but having been purged of its nauseating properties." The result is a drink fit for Indra – "Cleansed like a winning race horse, thou hast spilled thyself in the belly of Indra, O Soma!" (IX 85, 5cd).

For many, Wasson's conclusions may seem, um, a bit hard to swallow, but in the two decades since *Soma: Divine Mushroom of Immortality* was published, his theory has been widely recognized as the most credible regarding Soma's identity. And even at the time the book came out, it received laudatory reviews from two of the world's most respected anthropoligists, La Barre and Claude Levi-Strauss.

Levi-Strauss, in *L'Homme*, wrote: "Mr. R. G. Wasson advances a revolutionary hypothesis on the name of Soma, the implications of which are so widespread that ethnologists cannot leave the task of communicating it to Indian specialists only... Mr. Wasson's work establishes, in our opinion convincingly, that among all the candidatures put forward for representing Soma, *Amanita muscaria* is by far the most plausible."

La Barre, reviewing the book in *American Anthropologist*, applauded Wasson's "careful scholarship" and "his willingness to pursue the quest through the wide range of linguistics, archeology, folklore, philology, ethnobotany, plant ecology, human physiology and prehistory..." As time went by, La Barre's belief in Wasson's Soma findings increased so much that, in the essay he contributed to *The Sacred Mushroom Seeker,* he wrote: "That his solution is unquestionably correct – despite the miffed reluctance of some professional Sanskritists to follow him – is for me incontestably proven by the many doors to understanding opened by his discovery."

Robert Graves also reviewed Wasson's book. "The argument of Wasson's *Soma,*" he opined in *Atlantic Monthly,* "is as lucid as unanswerable; the illustrations are wonderful, the quotations are numerous and telling. I congratulate him on his feat."

Graves' opinion, however, was probably subject to some bias. Unlike Levi-Strauss and La Barre, he knew Wasson – in fact, he'd met and communicated with him often since the late 1940s, when they first corresponded regarding the sad, *Amanita*-related ending of poor old Claudius. Graves, as noted earlier, sent Wasson the Schultes article on Mexican mushroom use. Graves' enthusiasm for *Soma: Divine Mushroom of Immortality* at the time of its appearance would wane in later years – not because he came to deny Wasson's theory, but because he chaffed at the author's unwillingness to give him credit for his role in its development.

Graves, indeed, would claim that *he* first suggested to Wasson that Soma might have been AM. Whether that's true or not, Graves indisputably had plenty of original ideas about the mushroom's role in world myth and religion. In his own writings, as we shall see in the next chapter, Graves argued that AM lay behind much Greek and Celtic mythology – most intriguingly, perhaps, in the figure of the Greek god Dionysus.

FOOD OF THE GODS: ROBERT GRAVES AND THE AMBROSIA ACROSTIC

Like R. Gordon Wasson, Robert Graves was a headstrong maverick, though much more famous. His often controversial work and spiky personality received not only more attention during his life (1895-1985) but also more forbearance. He was, after all, a poet, and we all know how they can be.

Not merely a poet, though, by any means. Besides Graves' many books of verse, his experiences and defiantly eclectic interests also resulted in a frank World War I memoir, *Goodbye to All That*, the best-selling Roman-history novel, *I, Claudius* (and its sequel *Claudius the God*), a vivid description of *The Greek Myths* (which became a standard text on the subject), and more eccentric writings, including a colorfully convoluted book on Celtic myth, *The White Goddess*, as well as essays propounding daring views on a variety of subjects, including *Amanita muscaria*.

It had been a mushroom that eventually put an end to the life of the protagonist in Graves' two Claudius novels. Among the books' myriad readers was Wasson, who wrote Graves in 1949, inquiring about the identity of the emperor-killing species. This letter began a relationship – or, at least, association – that would last a little over a decade.

Graves not only replied (the answer being *Amanita phalloides*) but also subsequently offered further opinions and speculations regarding Wasson's mycological pursuits. This interest must have delighted Wasson. At the time, he had largely estranged himself from his fellow bankers, who called him "the mushroom man." Yet, with his amateur standing, he had gained little acceptance into the world of anthropologists or botanists. His only major publication on his fungal findings – the massive, privately published *Mushrooms, Russia and History* (written with his wife) – had sold only a few hundred copies.

Graves became the first prominent scholar to show interest in Wasson's work, to confirm some of his findings, and to suggest further areas of investigation. In fact – according to Graves, anyway – a tip from him led the Wassons to their *psilocybe* discoveries.

In his 1973 essay "The Two Births of Dionysus" Graves contended:

"It had been a chance piece of information that I passed on to him in the early Fifties that prompted him to investigate the mushroom oracles [meaning the *psilocybe*-imbibing healers] of Mexico."

Graves does not elaborate, but this is what Jay Stevens has to say about the matter in his *Storming Heaven*:

"In 1952 Graves came across a magazine story that mentioned the discovery of 'mushroom stones' at various archeological excavations in Guatemala and Mexico. The archeologists speculated that the stones had been objects of worship, or at least adoration, which suggested the existence in pre-Columbian times of a mushroom cult. Although the Wassons had planned to confine their study to Eurasia, they left for Mexico at the first available opportunity."

In November 1953, Wasson traveled to meet with Graves at the poet's adopted home in the Mediterranean island of Mallorca, and the two men remained friendly, according to Graves' biographer Martin Seymour-Smith, until the mid-1960s. For several years, theirs was a mutually beneficial association. "Wasson's interest in the psychological effects of hallucinogenic mushrooms and allied substances synthesized in the laboratory was to have a considerable influence on Graves towards the end of the fifties," Seymour-Smith wrote in *Robert Graves: His Life and Works*. "And Graves meanwhile helped build up Wasson's reputation." Wasson, Seymour-Smith surmises, "was awed by Graves' fame, but determined not to be overinfluenced by him. Sometimes his letters sound a slightly petulant note, perhaps arising from a resentment that he was a rich business man rather than a scholar – and thus forced to turn to qualified professionals and poets."

This attitude toward Graves – seeking his counsel yet holding him at arm's length – shaped the way Wasson acknowledged the poet's help; he simply didn't. The final straw for Graves, despite his approving review of the book, was *Soma: Divine Mushroom of Immortality*. Its entire length, including the 18-page index, held no mention of Graves. Wasson proved equally remiss of recognizing his one-time friend's aid elsewhere.

In a 1973 letter to two Swiss writers, Graves bemoaned this perceived mistreatment: "Wasson has been curiously abstemious in his mentions of me, considering that I first sent him the mushroom source in Mexico; introduced him to his sole European predecessors there; & sent him to another mushroom source in New Guinea, and so on and so on."

For evidence of Graves' own ingenious findings regarding mushrooms, and *Amanita muscaria* in particular, he encouraged the two writers to "read my 'Food for Centaurs,' a piece published by Doubleday 1960 in a book of that same name...."

In a later essay, "The Two Births of Dionysus," Graves made it clear what he was talking about: *He* had first realized that *Amanita muscaria* had something to do with Soma. And he mentioned this speculation to Wasson "at the time that I wrote my piece about Ambrosia, Soma's Greek counterpart, in the *Atlantic Monthly*."

Graves is referring to "Centaur's Food," which appeared in the *Atlantic Monthly*'s August 1956 issue, more than a decade before Wasson's *Soma* book. Reprinted in Graves' 1960 collection of essays *Food for Centaurs*, it is the first and most important of three short pieces Graves wrote about AM; the other two, "Mushrooms and Religion" and "The Two Births of Dionysus," can be found in his 1973 collection *Difficult Questions, Easy Answers*.

A MYTHOPHILE'S VIEW OF MYCOPHOBIA

"Centaur's Food" starts off with a history of how humans have divided into mycophiles (mushroom lovers; societies that actively hunt and use various species of edible mushrooms, becoming adept at distinguishing the harmful species) and mycophobes (those who avoid mushrooms entirely, or employ only one or a few store-bought species in their cuisine). Wasson is given full credit for his studies and theories. Then Graves goes on to offer his own hypotheses regarding the fly agaric and Greek myth; he argues – using a philological approach similar to that in *The White Goddess* (which has its own, though far more scattered, references to AM) – that the mushroom is the probable secret behind the mystery of "the food of the gods," Ambrosia, and the wild-natured god, Dionysus.

At the beginning of the essay, Graves reflects on his own culture's fear of wild mushrooms. He recalls a time from his childhood when he and his Welsh family visited Bavaria and some German cousins taught him and his sisters how to recognize several species of edible fungi. They all filled baskets with fungi and gave them to the cook, who added them to the evening's meal. After returning to Wales, he and his sisters spotted the same sorts of mushrooms and brought them to show to their mother. She reacted in horror, exclaiming: "Throw them away at once, dear children! They are deadly poison!"

Growing up, Graves found this disdain for wild mushrooms to be common among people of the British Isles. "Yet only three European mushrooms, *Amanita phalloides* and two other which experts alone can differentiate from it, are in fact lethal," he discovered. "You might as well refuse raspberries because the deadly-nightshade is poisonous; or apples because of the deadly manchineel."

Anthropologists have found that a culture's widespread disgust for things that are not actually harmful is usually a vestige of an old religious taboo. Paradoxically, the food or other substance was often forbidden to the general populace precisely because it was so highly prized by the elite. And even those who were allowed use of it had to follow strict regulations and rituals.

Tabooed substances are often associated with the Otherworld and sometimes with deities. That's particularly true of psychedelic mushrooms because they psychically open the door to that Otherworld. In "Centaur's Food," Graves cites Gordon and Valentina Wasson's *psilocybe* encounter in Mexico as an illustration.

However, long before humans settled in the New World and experimented with its psychedelic wonders, many had encountered another mushroom with transcendent powers somewhat similar to those of the *psilocybe* variety. This, of course, was *Amanita muscaria*. AM was native to the very European regions where the mushroom taboo was strongest: England, the Celtic countries of Ireland, Wales and Scotland, Germany, Scandinavia, Holland, northern France and Greece. In these areas, Graves notes, "this handsome, scarlet-capped mushroom with white spots was popularly held to be the deadliest fungus of all, [though] it had never been known to kill anyone in reasonably good health."

All of the societies inhabiting these lands were descendents of the Indo-Europeans – the very Aryans who had conquered India and brought with them their worship of the god/plant Soma. Europe's earliest Indo-European culture had settled in Greece, and Graves suspected (perhaps the better word is sensed, for he worked intuitively) vestiges of *Amanita muscaria* in Greek mythology, and investigated. His findings, summed up in "Centaur's Food," linked

AM with Dionysus and his famous festival, the Ambrosia – as well as with the "food of the gods" which took its name from this October celebration.

DIONYSUS AND AMBROSIA

Dionysus was, like his Roman counterpart Bacchus, god of intoxication, revelry and mystic illumination. He represented a connection between earth and heaven from the moment he was conceived – by the God of gods Zeus when he impregnated Semele, the mortal daughter of the dragon-killing Phoenician prince Cadmus. Six months into the pregnancy, Zeus, in one of his famous temper tantrums, slew Semele with a lightning bolt, but saved the infant, sewing it up in his own thigh, from which it was safely delivered three months later. The young, reborn Dionysus revived his mother and lifted her to the Olympic heights, where she changed her name to Thyone and became Queen of the Maenads – the wild women who presided over the ecstatic October festival called the Ambrosia, held in her son's honor.

Though the Ambrosia consumed at these festivities is generally defined as a "*food* of the gods," or a wine, or both, Graves pointed out that it was actually, like the practically synonymous Nectar, a liquid -- and that there have been almost as many guesses about what plant or plants that liquid was made from as guesses about Soma's identity.

He believed that something other than fermented grape juice accounted for Dionysian drunkenness.

The wild revels of the Maenads and the mystic illumination associated with Dionysus and Ambrosia, Graves argued, are much more sensibly explained by use of *Amanita muscaria* rather than the drinking of wine. He arrived at this conclusion through his knowledge of language – and his noted reliance on intuition.

Graves' intuited that there was something wrong with the most traditional recipe for Ambrosia – one that had it being a thick mixture of honey, water, olive oil, cheese, barley and unspecified fruit. The first thing that struck him odd about these ingredients was the mention of water. Perhaps, he thought, it was included because there was something special about the *number* of components.

Graves wrote down the Greek names for the six ingredients in their traditional order:

MELI (honey)

UDOR (water)

KARPOS (fruit)

ELAIOS (olive oil)

TUROS (cheese)

ALPHITA (pearl barley)

Take the first letter of each word, he wrote, and the recipe spells out *muketa* – the accusative form of the Greek word for mushroom, *mukes*.

Graves did the same thing with the ingredients for Nectar -- honey, water and fruit:

MELI

UDOR

KARPOS

This forms the acrostic *muk*, also suggesting *mukes*.

Finally, the poet wrote out the ingredients for the *kukeon* of the Eleusinian Mysteries. This libation, used in the initiation ceremony of the Dionysian secret society, was supposedly a mixture of mint-water and pounded barley:

MINTHAION

UDOR

KUKOMENON

ALPHITOIS

Thus spelling out *muka*, which, Graves says, was an earlier form of *mukes*.

THE TWO BIRTHS OF DIONYSUS

In his later essays "Mushrooms and Religion" and "The Two Births of Dionysus" Graves showed how the most curious aspect of ritual AM use may explain the "double-birth" of Dionysus.

The Greek god of intoxication, you'll remember, had been snatched by Zeus after being born from his earthly mother. The lord of all Greek deities encapsulated his son in his own thigh, from which he was "born again." This, Graves asserts, proves that "Dionysus was Ambrosia, as his Indian counterpart Agni was Soma."

Referring to Wasson's findings, Graves contends that the drinking of AM-infused urine practiced by the Korjaks of Siberia may have also figured into the Soma ritual of the Vedic priests, who, like their shamanic predecessors, might have used this method to "enjoy the same ecstasies" as the original imbiber. This "explains Dionysus's second birth from the thigh of his father Zeus and his subsequent release to worshippers in a stream of hallucinogenic urine."

Such speculation may seem far-fetched (as well as literally distasteful), even for Graves, but he's on more solid ground regarding taboos in Greek culture.

GREEK TABOOS ON THE USE OF MUSHROOMS

Graves admitted that most "learned scholars" will probably dismiss his interpretation "on the ground that not a single mushroom figures in the works of Homer, Hesiod, or even any of the Attic dramatists."

Yet, he surmised, this omission was in itself a clue, and "one would expect at least some admission that it existed: a metaphor, perhaps, drawn from its sudden rapid growth; or a term of comic abuse, as when Shakespeare disposes of a character in Troilus and Cressida with 'thou toadstool!'"

Graves believed that this strongly suggested "a conspiracy of silence – a conspiracy natural enough if mushrooms were the hallucinatory agents used by the mystagogues in the Eleusinian Mysteries (sacred to Demeter and Persephone and Dionysus) – the secret of which nobody ever blabbed in the course of all those centuries. There certainly was a secret: are we really expected to believe that the *epoptae*, or adepts, derived the visions that made them gasp for wonder from a soft drink of mint-flavoured barley-water?"

In "Mushrooms and Religion" Graves reiterates how the shunning of mushrooms spread from Greece and other early Aryan settlements throughout the rest of the continent – wherever Indo-European languages were spoken, including, of course, his own British Isles. However, he notes, "an unexplained relaxation of the taboo in England allowed the eating of white field mushrooms, though the most deadly European mushroom of all, the *Amanita phalloides*, with which Nero's stepfather the Emperor Claudius had been poisoned, was equally white and has often been mistaken for it."

This meant, Graves concluded, that it "is therefore reasonable to guess that the sacred mushroom originally protected by these taboos grew in forests, not in fields."

And he offers further evidence that the color of the sacred mushroom was scarlet. There was, he points out, "another curious taboo in force among the ancient Greeks. They were forbidden to eat any bright red food, such as lobsters, crabs, prawns and wild strawberries (which had no name because regarded as poisonous)."

If Graves' contention that *Amanita muscaria* played an important part in Greek mythology is a worthy one, isn't it possible – even probable – that the mushroom also played such a part in myths and legends of other European regions where it grows abundantly?

TWO OTHER 'SACRED MUSHROOM' AUTHORS

Robert Graves and R. Gordon Wasson may have been the first to link *Amanita muscaria* and the origin of certain mythologies and religions, but neither was the first author to have a book published specifically on the mushroom's possibly ancient role in human history. That honor goes to Andrija Puharich's *The Sacred Mushroom: Key to the Door of Eternity*, published in 1959.

Puharich's book deals mostly with ESP (extrasensory perception) experiments he held with a supposed psychic sculptor named Harry Stone. After spontaneously falling into a trance, Stone would speak and write in Ancient Egyptian. Identifying himself as Ra Ho Tep, a highborn priest who lived 4600 years ago, Stone indicated in several ways that AM was employed in the religious rituals of ancient Egypt. Puharich claims that renowned author Aldous Huxley attended one of these sessions.

The Sacred Mushroom is a fairly diverting read, but it never received much attention or respect from scholars. One reason is that Puharich does not support the AM-Egypt theory with much more than Stone's obviously questionable presentation, which might have been simply an act. Another reason is Puharich's deep involvement years later with another alleged psychic, Uri Geller, whose paranormal claims were eventually disclosed and ridiculed as ruses.

Another book with a similar title, *The Sacred Mushroom and the Cross* by John M. Allegro, was greeted with more reaction from scholars – at least in Allegro's native England. However, almost all of that reaction was negative.

Published in 1970, Allegro's book sold reasonably well in Britain and America – a Bantam paperback appeared in 1971. Much of the initial notice was based on the author's reputation. He was a lecturer in Old Testament and Inter-Testamental Studies at the University of Manchester. And he was the first British representative on the international team of linguists and scholars appointed to examine the Dead Sea Scrolls and prepare them for publication.

It was in this latter role that Allegro's eventually notorious rebelliousness became demonstrated, as he increasingly broke away from the rest of the team and protested many of their methods. He wrote the first popular book on the Scrolls.

Allegro's prickly approach to the Scrolls was merely a warm-up for the controversy he caused with *The Sacred Mushroom and the Cross*. In this work he proposed nothing less than that the New Testament was a coded text disguising the practices of a long-established Middle Eastern mushroom cult. He claimed that Jesus Christ himself was merely the personification of *Amanita muscaria*.

The proof that Allegro presented was almost entirely linguistic. He claimed that a great many words and phrases in the New Testament – and some in the Old Testament as well – had mushroom-meaning roots. Many of these, he tried to demonstrate, were related to far older Sumerian words, showing the antiquity of the cult. As if this were not enough to gall Christians, he also repeatedly claimed that the New Testament often stressed the sexual symbolism of AM.

Christians weren't the only ones upset. Several linguists publicly denounced Allegro's methodology, and no one prominent in the field backed up his contentions. On top of that, *The Sacred Mushroom and the Cross*, unlike Puharich's and Wasson's books, was not an easy read. Still, while it's hard to make one's way through the bog of Allegro's reasoning, his book remains a remarkable and definitely unique addition to AM literature.

PART FIVE
THE SOLUTION

SHAMANIC SUCCESSION AND THE GRAIL LEGEND

Jessie Weston came close to completely solving the mystery of the Grail legend, but she was born too soon. Had she lived 50 or 60 years later, and had she been able to learn what R. Gordon Wasson revealed about Soma, that information might have been all she needed to determine the true nature of the reality behind the myth.

Similarly, if Weston had learned what we know now about humanity's archetypal healers, the shamans – if she, especially, had been able to read Mircea Eliade's groundbreaking study *Shamanism: Archaic Techniques of Ecstasy* – she would have surely seen the connections with the Grail stories, and would have been delighted to find just how correct her intuitions were about the knight/healer factor.

It is far easier today to perceive the following possibilities:

That the Grail legend is a story symbolizing shamanic succession and the sacred nature of the Euro-Asian shaman's most useful implement.

That the knights in the original, oral versions of the legend, especially Perceval and Gawain, may have represented exceptional young men considered and tested for the position of shaman.

And that the King(s) of the Grail castle symbolized the elder, ailing shaman who evaluated and initiated the candidates who might take his place.

SEARCH FOR A SHAMAN

In societies that depend on shamans the replacement of the dying healer/prophet/poet with someone possessing a rare combination of knowledge, intuition, courage and dementia is of the utmost importance.

As Eliade indicates, a number of ritualized tests, procedures and initiations are devised to determine which of the tribe's several candidates possessed true magical attributes.

Knowledge of this process was passed down orally from generation to generation. The story of the Grail descends from this oral tradition, with the rituals couched in metaphorical terms to keep their true meaning disguised from outsiders. The details became blurred and altered through generations, much like a centuries-long game of "Simon Says."

Though several knights witness or seek the Grail throughout these tales, Perceval and Gawain appear to be the most consequential. The other, less successful knights in the stories (Galahad, Bors, et al.) may have represented the shamanic candidates who fail the tough, baffling tests.

Gawain's original role and eventual fate are both difficult to determine. Particularly intriguing and frustrating is the way he hops in and out of Chrétien's unfinished story. Gawain possesses some qualities that indicate success - mainly, healing attributes. More often, he is portrayed in a way that would seem to mark him a failure; he's callous, vengeful, lustful.

Of course, Perceval is callous at first, too, and worse - particularly in his rough treatment of the woman from whom he steals a ring. However, in both Chrétien and Wolfram (where, of course, his name is spelled Parzifal) he exhibits more characteristics of the potential shaman than any other Arthurian protagonist.

Perceval grows up in a forest. He is portrayed as a foolish youth. Upon seeing knights for the first time he mistakes them for angels. Sent out into the big bad world by his mother, he wears rustic clothing and is considered not quite right in the head by people who encounter him. (The first card in the Tarot pack, The Fool, provides the perfect image.)

It may seem odd, but these are precisely the qualities that would have marked him as a potential shaman.

Regarding practices in two Siberian societies (the Buryat and the Altains), Eliade wrote: "In the case of hereditary shamanism, the souls of the ancestral shamans choose a young man in the family; he becomes absent-minded and dreamy, loves solitude, and has prophetic visions and sometimes seizures that make him unconscious."

However, Eliade added, the potential shaman is sometimes unrelated to the elder shaman, especially if the latter had no offspring, or if the traditions of the tribe dictate otherwise. "The office of medicine man is not hereditary among a considerable number of primitive people, whom it is unnecessary to cite here. This means that all over the world magico-religious powers are held to be obtainable either spontaneously (sickness, dream, chance encounter with a source of 'power,' etc.) or deliberately (quest)."

Speaking of another Siberian tribe (the Yurak-Samoyed), Eliade stated: "Toward the approach of maturity the candidate begins to have visions, sings in his sleep, likes to wander in solitude, and so on; after this incubation period he attaches himself to an old shaman..." The elder "transmits the secret knowledge to [the candidate]."

POSSESSED BY THE SPIRIT

Consider, too, keeping the Grail hero in mind, these other components of the shamanic succession as described by Eliade:

"However selected, a shaman is not recognized as such until after he has received two kinds of teaching: (1) ecstatic (dreams, trances, etc.) and (2) traditional (shamanic techniques, names and functions of the spirits, mythology and genealogy of the clan, secret language, etc.).

"Instruction plays an important role, but it does not begin until the first ecstatic experience.

"Thus it may happen that candidates run away to the mountains and remain there seven days or longer, feeding on animals 'caught...directly with their teeth,' and returning to the village dirty, bleeding, with torn clothes and hair disheveled, 'like wild people.' It is only some ten days later that the candidate begins babbling incoherent words. Then an old shaman cautiously asks him questions; the candidate (more precisely, the 'spirit' possessing him) becomes angry, and finally designates the shaman who is to offer the sacrifices to the gods and prepare the ceremony of initiation and consecration.

"All of this constitutes "a 'quest' for powers by the candidate."

THE TWO KINGS

Chrétien places two kings in the Grail Castle, a curious and confusing situation about which Emma Jung and Marie Louise Von Franz had some insightful things to say in their *The Grail Legend*.

After a discussion of Perceval's relationship to his mother and of the unconscious as the "realm of the mothers," Jung and von Franz noted:

"At any rate, Perceval does not find a world of mothers in the Grail Castle. On the contrary, he finds a world of 'fathers,' who, however, belong on the distaff side. The Rich Fisher, as the master of the Grail Castle is called, is a cousin of Perceval, according to Chrétien, while the mysterious old king to whom the Host is brought in the Grail is his uncle, *a brother of his mother*, [italics theirs] to whom the meaning of a 'spiritual father' is frequently given in primitive societies."

Jung and von Franz detect in these family ties an element that brings us right back to Weston's intuitions about a connection between the Grail legend and ancient rites.

"[I]t is always -- with the exception of the Grail Bearer, who may be taken as an anima figure – father figures whom the hero meets in the Grail Castle."

Consider the aboriginal societies whose sacred and hierarchal traditions come through faintly but hauntingly in the Grail legend. In such societies, the chieftain might be succeeded with few complications by his son or another relative. But the selection of the tribe's shaman – its doctor, poet and often much else – was a trickier matter.

After all, many a realm, ancient and historic, has survived the rule of a physically or even mentally infirm leader. But in prehistoric clans it was crucial for the shaman to not only possess the "secret knowledge" of healing herbs and such, but also to *be* possessed by healing spirits – or know how to become so possessed. It is hard to comprehend this in our age of the rational physician as an ideal, but the medicine man of our ancestors needed to be demented in certain respects – to be a "wise fool" capable of true magic.

As we have seen, the elder shaman attempted to find such a wise fool by putting young candidates through ritualized tests and initiations. These procedures – the rules of the game – were, like other important traditions, passed down carefully and orally from generation to generation. And the most sacred of these traditions were transmitted in guarded, coded, often metaphorical form, so that it would be difficult for outsiders to learn their exact nature.

The Grail stories are distorted fragments of such oral traditions. As Jung and von Franz wrote concerning the Grail succession:

"This concept of handing over and taking over has something very archaic about it. It suggests a time before there was any writing by which knowledge could be preserved."

MARKALE ON SHAMANISM AND THE GRAIL

Jean Markale noted a connection between the Grail legend and shamanism in his *The Grail: The Celtic Origins of the Sacred Icon*.

In the last chapter of his book, "The Meaning of the Quest" discusses the quest as "perilous adventure," representing the hero's need to learn how to confront psychological "monsters and demons" and how various "hermits or mysterious women... guide the heroes and aid them in vanquishing the terrors born from this materialization of fantasies."

Then he asserts: "In a similar vein it is easy to see the journey of the apprentice shaman in the trials of the Quest, the individual who, under the guidance of a master present either in reality of thought, will be forced to awareness of the dangers he runs every instant of his wandering. There are numerous analogies between the different versions of the quest and the stories of the ecstatic journeys of humans. The symbolism is often the same, and in the end the goal is similar: the shaman in fact wishes to heal a sufferer from illness by going in search of the patient's soul in the dark depths of the Otherworld. The aim of this intervention is regeneration, just as are the actions of the Grail hero."

This would seem to lead to the implication of an ultimate shamanic source for the Grail legend, but Markale senses this and immediately, if inexplicably, refuses to go down that path.

"But I don't mean to imply that *The Quest of the Holy Grail* as we know it is a souvenir of shamanism, even if the elements issued from a primal shamanism are obvious in the beliefs and rituals of Celtic druidism. Only the methods and symbolism are parallel. It seems that the Quest is more a pure, truly scientific search than a healing or simple driving away of wicked spirits."

And he leaves it at that. While I'm disappointed and perplexed at Markale's unwillingness to take the shamanism-Grail link to what seems to be its natural outcome, I was thrilled to see that, subsequently in this final chapter, he views the story of Finn and the Salmon of Wisdom as "key" to solving the Grail puzzle.

We will see just how right he was about this "key" – even though he didn't know exactly why. That famous Celtic tale, along with the two "fishiest" matters mentioned in the Grail legend itself – namely the Fisher King (aka the Rich Fisher) and the story of Brons, the fish and the Grail – lead straight to the heart of the mystery, and to the secret of what the Grail vessel was meant to hold.

THE FISHER KING AND THE FISH

A deep dive into the mystery of the Grail legend reveals that there's definitely – and literally – something "fishy" going on here.

First and foremost, there is the curious name of the Fisher King. In *Le Conte du Graal*, the oldest known Grail story, there is no explanation for this title other than the one provided to Perceval by the maiden he encounters soon after leaving the mysterious castle.

"Did you lie then at the dwelling of the rich Fisher King?" she asks him.

"I do not know if he is fisherman or king," Perceval replies, "but he is very rich and courteous." The maiden assures him that his host is a king, one who had been maimed in battle. "A javelin wounded him through the two thighs." The wound will not heal, she explains, and the old man can no longer mount a horse. Instead, he finds diversion in fishing.

"Therefore, he is called the Fisher King."

Later in Chrétien's tale we are presented with the decidedly odd statement of the hermit who warns Perceval against mistakenly concluding that the Grail contains a fish. What makes this utterance so thoroughly strange is that no such connection has been mentioned earlier – by Perceval or anyone else.

And then there is the strange incident in Robert de Boron's *Joseph of Arimathea* that directly connects the Grail with a fish.

Joseph, who has taken possession of the Grail (in this tale, the cup from the Last Supper) prepares a ritual meal surrounding it. He instructs his brother-in-law, Brons, to catch a fish. After the fish is caught, Joseph tells Brons to place it beside the Grail on a special table that has been constructed for the service. Brons is later designated "the Rich Fisher" by Joseph, who dispatches him to Britain with the Grail.

Such references to fish in the Grail legend are striking and bizarre, even for a set of tales filled with curious and confusing occurrences. These ichthyological inklings have reminded some Arthurian scholars of the fish symbolism in Celtic mythology – especially the role of the sacred salmon in tales such as that of Finn and the Salmon of Wisdom, as we shall see in the next chapter.

If we consider each of these elements in more detail, we will see how they all point to a solution to the mystery of the Grail.

THE FISHER KING

"This name has caused much speculation and has yet to be clearly or satisfactorily explained," Emma Jung and Marie-Louise Von Franz wrote of the Fisher King in their *The Grail Legend*. The authors did not buy the maiden's explanation that the name comes from the king's fishing. "This seems unlikely, since he is regularly called 'The Fisher King' even when he is not in the least concerned with angling."

Other Grail scholars are also skeptical. A widespread view holds that the ruler's name probably has more to do with that curious episode in Robert de Boron's *Joseph of Arimathea*.

Finding this passage particularly significant, Weston wrote: "Robert de Boron is the only writer who gives a clear, and tolerably reasonable, account of why the guardian of the Grail bears the title of Fisher King; in other cases, such as the poems of Chrétien and Wolfram, the name is connected with his partiality for fishing, an obviously *post hoc* addition."

In *Joseph*, she recounts, "we are told how, during the wanderings of that holy man and his companions in the wilderness, certain of the company fell into sin. By the command of God, Brons, Joseph's brother-in-law [whose name is spelled Bron or Hebron in some versions], caught a Fish, which, with the Grail, provided a mystic meal of which the unworthy cannot partake... Henceforward Brons was known as 'The Rich Fisher'..."

That solution suits Jung and Von Franz, too. "In Robert de Boron, Joseph's brother-in-law Brons catches a fish which is put on the table beside the Grail. This is why the guardian of the Grail is known as the Fisher King."

THE DIVINE PRESENCE

The noted Celtic scholar Jean Markale, summarizing Robert's tale in *The Grail: Celtic Origins of the Sacred Icon*, wrote that because "sin has slipped into the community," Joseph, "on God's orders, establishes a ritual: the members of the community must join together for a fraternal meal – analogous to that of the first Christians

– around a table in the middle of which sits the holy vessel, with a fish caught by King Bron [Markale's spelling and designation] right next to it.

"All of this is obviously a recollection of the Last Supper," Markale surmised, "and reveals Robert de Boron's intention to emphasize the divine presence, according to the theological trends of his era...

"Joseph lays down precise rules concerning this feast of the holy vessel. Only those touched by the grace of God are admitted to this table... The guests admitted to this table experience an indescribable joy, which is the ecstatic exaltation obtained from receiving, quite in the tone of Cistercian theology. Those not welcome at this table are therefore reprobates, people who God doesn't deign to touch with his grace. And these individuals understand nothing of what is taking place there..."

As we shall soon see, there is every reason to suspect that the ecstasy experienced at this mystic meal, as with that at certain earlier meals in other cultures, involved the practice of a ritual employing a psychedelic sacrament.

BRON AND BRAN

Most Grail scholars have noted the strong possibility of a connection between Brons, aka Brons, and the Celtic god Bran.

As Markale put it: "The name Bron has inspired much discussion... Is it an abbreviation of Hebron or a Celtic borrowing? In the latter case Bron means 'breast, height, eminence, nipple, or hillock,' which permits certain commentaries concerning the Grail itself. In addition the name Bron could very well be a variation of Bran, who is a well known figure in Welsh mythology... This Bran, surnamed Bendigeit (the Blessed) appears in the second branch of the *Mabinogion* as the owner of a strange Cauldron of Resurrection, and his severed head presides over a Feast of Immortality with obvious similarities to the Grail Feast."

NO 'PIKE, LAMPREY OR SALMON'

Let us now return to *Le Conte du Graal* and those strange words spoken by the hermit to Perceval regarding the nature of the Grail – that it serves no "pike, lamprey or salmon."

For those who might have skipped my earlier summary of *Le Conte du Graal*, let us recap this part of the story.

Following Chrétien's odd tangent into the adventures of Gawain, we rejoin Perceval five years after his visit to the Grail castle. We are told that he has had many adventures upon his quest to learn the meaning of what he observed at the castle, but has come no closer to an answer.

On a Good Friday, a procession of knights and ladies who are observing the holy day reprimand him for not doing so. Perceval, who has lost all remembrance of God and the church, follows them to a holy man's chapel where Mass is to be held. Giving confession to this hermit, Perceval tells him of his failure to aid the Fisher King.

When the hermit learns Perceval's name, he informs him that he is his uncle (his mother's brother) and that "he who is served from [the Grail] is my brother; the Rich Fisher is his son, and your mother was our sister."

Perceval, then, suddenly learns not only that there are *two* kings in the Grail castle, but that he is related to both. The elder king is, like the hermit, a maternal uncle, and thus Perceval's cousin.

The hermit then immediately adds: "Do not imagine that perchance the Grail contains pike, lamprey or salmon," that is, a fish. "No, it is only by the Host [a single Mass-wafer] that is brought to him in this Grail that the holy man maintains life!"

The Grail is so holy and the old king so spiritual, the hermit adds, that the reclusive fellow has stayed alive for fifteen years on this one-a-day diet.

Most scholars have expressed total bafflement with this out-of-nowhere "no fish" business. Could it be a possible indication that in the lost source material used by Chrétien – or that material's own antecedents – the Grail procession included a fish, one connected with the carving dish and the "*graal*" in a fashion similar to the fish and Grail of the Brons story?

If so, this element was excised by the re-tellers (probably along with a good deal else), because it seemed too incongruous. *Or because it indicated something forbidden*.

Now, though, we can understand what that "pike or salmon" represented. It is the very thing represented in much of the fish symbolism that runs throughout world mythology, particularly Indo-European mythology.

THE SECRET BEHIND FISH SYMBOLISM

The prevalence of fish symbolism has long intrigued religious and mythological authorities. To a great extent, most have concluded, the symbol stood for the unknown, the unconscious, all that lies beyond man's knowledge. However, it often seems to have signified something more specific – some esoteric secret.

Joseph Campbell begins his landmark 730-page work *The Masks of God: Creative Mythology* with a discussion of fish symbolism that leads us toward the revelation of this secret.

He begins by describing the figures on an Orphic sacramental bowl of gold, one discovered in Romania in the 19th Century, which he found particularly suggestive:

"Orpheus the Fisherman is here shown with his fishing pole, the line wound around it, a mesh bag in his elevated hand, and a fish lying at his feet. One thinks of Christ's words to his fishermen apostles, Peter, James and John: 'I shall make you fishers of men'; but also of the Fisher King of the legends of the Grail: and with this latter comes the idea that the central figure of the vessel, seated with a chalice in her hands, may be a prototype of the Grail Maiden in the castle to which the questing knight was directed by the Fisher King."

Campbell goes on to point out the prevalence of fish symbolism in world mythology. The intriguing fish-god Orpheus is just one representative of the "ever-dying, ever-living god... the consumer and the consumed... Of old he was known as Dionysus-Orpheus-Bacchus; earlier still Dumuzi-Tammuz..."

A central element of fish symbolism is the sacramental fish-meal. Jessie Weston believed that it had something to do with the Grail procession, with its plate, chalice, table, knives and – discarded by later re-tellers – fish.

"Fish," she remarked, "play an important part in Mystery Cults, as being the 'holy' food."

That holy food, we now can understand, was *Amanita muscaria*.

THE FISH-LIKE FIGURE

Some of the fish-like features of AM and other amanitas have long been obvious to mycologists, who have made these characteristics part of their science's terminology.

For instance, mycologists call the area underneath the cap of this mushroom (and many others) "gills." And they often refer to the white spots, flakes or splotches on AM's red cap as "scales."

The correlations don't stop there. Consider the form of a fish turned vertically, so that it stands on its tail. (As Jung points out in *Aion*, his study of the relationship between fish symbolism and his concept of the Self, this is how fish are often represented in ancient mythological illustrations.) Compare that image to a photograph of a specimen of *Amanita muscaria* in which the crown has just begun to separate from the stem, and the top has not yet flattened.

Note, then:

The crowning cap of the mushroom is comparable to the fish's head.

The gills are positioned exactly at the partition between head (cap) and body (stem, etc.), just as they are on a fish.

The stem corresponds to the fish's body, with the ring around it resembling top and bottom fins when viewed from this position, leading to...

The widening base, which resembles from this angle a fish's tail.

Users of *Amanita muscaria* in stream-filled northern forests from Siberia to Britain would have easily noted the similarities between fish and mushrooms. Both gifts of nature were of the highest importance to these people – especially the shamans who employed the sacred mushroom and invented the oral poetry that praised it and preserved knowledge of it.

However, one fish in particular would have worked as a near-perfect symbol for AM. And it is none other than the fish considered, not coincidentally, sacred in Celtic mythology and connected there with the gaining of supernatural wisdom – the king of fishes, the salmon.

THE SACRED SALMON: AM IN DISGUISE

Jean Markale states in *The Grail: The Celtic Origins of the Sacred Icon* that the "symbolism of the salmon is extremely important" in Celtic mythology, where, he notes, it is "a sacred animal." This is largely because "if it lives the greater part of its life in estuaries, it is capable of returning to the source" – thus symbolizing in powerfully magical form the circle of life.

At the end of his book on the Grail, Markale focuses on the fish symbolism in Celtic salmon tales – and what he sees as a link between them and the figure of the Fisher King.

"The Fisher King is the master of the fish, the Salmon of Knowledge and Abundance," Markale opines. "This is his most ancient role in Celtic mythology and all the later explanations can't change a whit of this fundamental aspect of the character. The fish is, symbolically, the most archaic of creatures, since all living things derive from the mutation of a primordial aquatic entity that lived in the vast oceans of the world's beginning. The Welsh text of *Culhwch and Olwen* made it the oldest animal in the entire world, the one who consequently knows all mysteries and secrets."

Noting that *Culhwch and Olwen* is the earliest known manuscript of Arthurian literature, Markale sees it "at the very heart of the Quest for the Holy Grail." And what makes it so is the role of a particularly marvelous salmon, one that "is supposed to know the secrets that no one else knows."

THE FINN/SALMON STORY: 'KEY TO THE GRAIL QUEST'

But it is the Finn tale that Markale finds to be most illuminating. "The key to the Grail Quest is in this initiation of Finn that is due to the salmon of Fec." Markale connects this inspirational salmon to the fish the Fisher King seeks in the river near his castle, and to more: "The blood of Christ is a food for the same reasons as the flesh of the salmon given to the eagle, for the same reasons as the salmon of Fec ingested by Finn Mac Cumail, and for the same reasons as the fish allegedly caught by Bron."

Markale then asks this question: "In truth, the Grail can contain anything, in other words all or nothing. Why couldn't it hold the salmon?"

As we have seen, he did not go on from there to determine anything like my conclusions when he wrote his book on the Grail (which was published in France in 1982, though not in the U.S. until 1999). He speaks of shamanism a little, yes, but not of magic mushrooms. Instead, Markale suggests, "this mythic salmon represents the primordial individual. Hence the true object, within the context of the Quest, is the rediscovery and embodiment of this individual in the final stage of a long personal experience."

Of course, if he had gone down the same path of thought that I have, his book would have taken on quite a different shape, while mine would have been largely or completely superfluous. So I appreciate his brilliant observations, as I do Jessie Weston's, but I also appreciate that I'm lucky both stopped their fishing about in the Grail legend before they came upon what I have hooked.

While AM is nicely symbolized as a fish, it is most aptly and ingeniously represented as a salmon.

A MOST SUITABLE SYMBOL

The salmon symbolizes *Amanita muscaria* better than any other fish, because:

The nutritious, treasured flesh of the salmon has a color very close to that of the more orange-tinged fly amanites.

The female salmon fights frantically to lay its eggs, its skin turning a deep red when it reaches its goal. After laying its eggs, the fish dies. This is wonderfully analogous to the way the mushroom bursts upward from its own "egg," shines briefly in scarlet shamelessness (actually spreading its own progeny, its spores, to the wind), and then quickly decays and disappears.

This cyclical, annual journey of the salmon upriver relates beautifully to the also-amazing, regenerative manner in which AM rises, seemingly disappears, and is "magically" born again the next year.

Thus the story of Finn and the Salmon of Knowledge connote, like the Grail legend, the "proving" of the young shamanic initiate and his worthiness to use the red-topped, consciousness-altering mushroom.

WHAT THE GRAIL SYMBOLS SYMBOLIZE

Just as the Grail legend's accounts of ailing kings and aspiring knights represent a tradition of shamanic succession, the various forms of the Grail symbolize the shaman's sacrament and implements.

Because the rituals connected with this sacrament and its implements were even more secret than the methods of replacing the dying shaman with the winning candidate, their true nature could never be clearly depicted in the oral tradition of the tales that became the Grail legend. They were never known to the Europeans who wrote out romances based on those tales.

Yet the symbolic forms of the Grail in those romances remained close enough to the real objects they represented so that the connections never became thoroughly obscured.

Each of the symbols in the original stories – chalice, dish, bowl, sword, lance, stone – stood either for something that held or cut the holy sacrament during the shaman's rituals, or for *Amanita muscaria* itself.

Throughout most of the adventures the Grail is something that contains the consumable sacrament. "What is clear is that the Grail is connected with food," Cavendish writes. "It is a serving vessel of some kind. It carries the Mass-wafer which is the only nourishment of the aged Grail King and it is associated with the fine feast which Perceval and the Fisher King enjoy. It is not part of the feast in *[Le Conte du Graal*], but it passes before Perceval's eyes with each course of the banquet. The connection with food, and with especially enjoyable and satisfying food, is one of the Grail's most constant characteristics in the stories."

Yet the Grail is no *mere* vessel, Cavendish notes. It is "clearly no ordinary object. It is surrounded with mystery, it is holy and it emanates blazing light... The Grail is linked with the sun, which from very early times all over the world has been revered as the creator and sustainer of life on earth. Another old and widespread theme is that the sun's reappearance in the morning after its disappearance at sunset is a symbol of life renewed after death."

We have seen, through Wasson, how this sun/AM connection also lay behind the figure of Soma.

In the original stories, Geoffrey Ashe writes in *King Arthur's Avalon: The Story of Glastonbury*, "the passages depicting [the Grail's] apparitions are often so curt, so cryptic, so allusive, that they have the air of being hints at matters known to the author and to some of his readers but not described."

Ashe then quotes Sebastian Evans' reflections on these matters: "We feel as we read that the words employed are intended to convey some deeper meaning than the fiction bears on the face of it. The romance is more than a romance. It is also a secret written in cipher. Its mysticism is as marked as its mystery. Throughout, there is a continual suggestion of hidden meanings, a recurrent insistence on things seen as types and symbols of things unseen."

Ashe continues: "Behind all these modes of the Grail there is a single thought which all the romancers are variously driving at. The dream which haunts their imagination is that somewhere on earth there was once a certain Object. It was the Ark of the New Covenant; de Boron says so explicitly. It was a visible pledge, *the* visible pledge, of God's friendship toward mankind. More is meant here than a vague benevolence or goodwill."

Expounding on this idea of some profound thing signifying an offer of friendship from God to man, Ashe alludes to the dangers that are inherent in the Grail quest along with its potential rewards – risks reminiscent of those involved in partaking of psychedelic drugs. "Friendship, particularly the friendship of the great, can be tragically demanding and disruptive. The Grail atmosphere sometimes recalls the peremptory invitations in the parable of the Suppers {*Luke* xiv. 16-24). A knight who achieves the Quest may wreck his life doing it. But the Grail rewards him with the priceless assurance: God is there, God's hand reaches towards us through the cruelty and indifference of the world, God wills that human beings shall enter into the ranks of the blest. Whatever the sacrifice, the assurance is worth it."

"Such a meaning," Ashe believes, "is easily abstracted from the life-giving talismans and relics belonging to various levels of the myth."

Let us now examine and explain those Grail symbols one by one, beginning with the vessel forms.

THE GRAIL VESSEL: THE CHALICE AND THE CARVING PLATTER

"A special symbolic value belongs to the chalice in which the God-Man perpetually offers himself," Ashe writes. "It contains the Incarnation and the Atonement, by which God draws Man to himself. It contains the sacraments by which God sanctifies and enlightens him."

It is fitting, if somewhat misleading (as it should be with any smartly conceived symbol), that the most popular conception of the Grail should be the chalice. This ornate cup cleverly represents *both* the vessel that held a potion made from *Amanita muscaria* and the shape of the mushroom itself.

To understand why this is so, simply look at pictures of several medieval chalices. You will see that the most typical sort is topped by the cup holding the liquid. This part is similar to the shape of the mushroom's crowning cap in its next-to-last form (before it flattens out). And it is usually engraved with intricate patterns or figures suggesting nature's ornamentation of the AM cap with a swirl of variously shaped white spots or scales.

Below the cup the chalice narrows down to a stem. This exactly parallels the stem that supports the mushroom's top. In addition, the medieval chalice's stem is usually augmented with a protruding ring about midway down – just like the ring around the stem of the *Amanitas*. Finally, the chalice widens again at the bottom, just as AM widens at its bulbous volva.

I'm not saying that chalices weren't shaped similarly before they were chosen to represent the secret sacrament of the Grail story. The widening base, of course, enabled one to safely set the vessel down on a table, and the ring around the middle of the stem facilitated handling of the cup. What I am saying is that this sort of vessel offered a ready-made symbol for AM when one was needed.

As you'll remember, though, the earliest Grail story, Chrétien's, does not describe the Grail as a chalice. In fact, it does not describe it as any particular object. And, as you'll also recall, scholars believe Chrétien's "graal" referred to the Old French word *gradalis*, which was a serving dish, or platter.

In *Le Conte du Graal*, the "graal" is followed by a silver carving dish (*tailleor*), the final item of the procession. This form lends itself to an

AM interpretation just as handily as the chalice, and for the same doubled reasons – through form and function.

The shape of the large, round serving dish would be identical with the final form of the fly amanite's cap, after it has transformed from the more bulbous cap to a flattened appearance. And the platter would be the sacred implement upon which AM would be carved into edible portions or chopped for brewing into the liquid that the chalice would hold.

It is also interesting to note that in one of the early Grail tales, *Perlesvaus*, King Arthur himself goes to the Grail castle and perceives the Grail assuming five forms. We are only told what one of these forms, the chalice, is. Could these five forms represent the various stages of the growing *Amanita muscaria*?

In any case, let us now turn to the Grail implements which would perform the carving upon the carving platter.

THE SWORD AND THE LANCE

After Perceval enters the Grail castle in *Le Conte du Graal*, he is immediately presented with objects representing the secret of the strange place – and indicating the significance of his role in something related to that secret.

Four squires drape the visitor in "a scarlet mantle, fresh and new" and take him to a square hall. Then, just after the lord of the castle has risen from his place before the fire and begun to talk to Perceval, a squire enters carrying a sword. Noting that this sword was made "of a steel so hard that it couldn't be broken save by one danger alone, known only to he who had forged and tempered it," the lord presents it to Perceval, declaring that the weapon was "destined" to be his.

During this odd introduction to the Fisher King, Perceval is made aware, too, of this master's crippling injury. Markale sees in these early events at the castle a definite indication of a blood relationship. "It is obvious that the Fisher King's wound is reminiscent of the wound of Perceval's own father, emphasized by the fact that there are bonds of kinship between the two men. The Fisher King is – although the hero doesn't know this yet – his uncle, or his cousin, the text isn't very clear on this point. In any event when Perceval finds himself at the Grail Castle he also finds himself at home with this family, with his clan. This is the reason he is given the sword that is destined to be broken in a predetermined situation."

Markale also associates this weapon with other "magic or holy swords" in the Celtic tradition. "It brings to mind Excalibur ('hard cutting' in Welsh), the magic sword of Arthur that corresponds to the Irish Caladbolg, the sword of the god Nuada of the Silver Hand that 'no one could escape when drawn from its warrior's scabbard and which no one could withstand.' In addition it would burn the hand of anyone who took hold of it without just cause. It is also reminiscent of Durandal, Siegfried's sword, and, of course, the Sword of the Strange Belt that plays such an important role in late tales of the Quest."

Another squire enters. He holds a white lance and walks between the fire and the two men. The point of the lance emits "a drop of red blood." Heeding advice he'd previously been given about talking too much, Perceval refrains from asking about any of this.

Perceval may restrain his curiosity, but for almost 800 years people have pondered what these odd objects and events mean. Definitely, some meaning is being conveyed. Now we can determine what that meaning was.

The most telling symbol is the lance. Besides its extraordinary emission of a drop of blood – "red blood," Chrétien writes, just in case we might miss the significance of the color – there is the highly unusual color of the lance itself to consider. It is white.

And so we have here, with a white shaft and reddened top, an object that strongly suggests AM's white stem (sometimes itself called a shaft) and often blood-red cap.

The fly agaric was the most secret and holy agent in the European and Asian shaman's pharmacy, the key to his ability to heal the ailing. Does the lance have any healing properties in the Grail legend?

Not in Chrétien – there its purpose is clouded. However, in at least two subsequent early versions, as Jung and von Franz note, the lance "is not only responsible for the wounding of the Grail King but, like Arthur's Excalibur, also serves to heal the wound it has inflicted. When the bleeding spear in Wolfram's *Parzival* is held to the wound, it is supposed to draw out the poison and relieve Anfortas' pain. In the *Quests*, Galahad heals the King by spreading blood from the lance over the wound."

Like the lance, the sword that is quickly passed on to Perceval represents both the sacred mushroom and the implement with which it is dismembered.

To understand how the weapon suggests the shape of AM, simply think of a medieval sword stuck straight down into the ground (or into a stone, as Excalibur is). In this position, the blade signifies the mushroom's stem, and the hilt resembles its cap. In addition, the sword stands for the sharp knife that the shaman would use to separate the chemical-imbued cap from the relatively impotent stem and volva.

The magic mushroom, like the magic sword, is destined to be broken up. Only then will it unleash its powers. And as for the description of this weapon in later Grail- legend versions as "The Sword of the Strange Belt," note that AM has its own "strange belt" ringing the middle of its stem.

LAPIS EXILIS: THE GRAIL STONE

The four treasures of Tuatha De Danann, the gods of ancient Irish myth, included the unconquerable sword of the god Lug (or Lugh) and a magic spear. The other two treasures were the cauldron of the divine being Dagda and the Lia Fail, the Stone of Destiny. We have already seen how cauldron, sword and spear relate to *Amanita muscaria*. Now we shall see how the wonder-working mushroom is also symbolized as a magic stone.

Much as the freeing of Excalibur from a stone showed that Arthur was its rightful, royal owner in ancient Britain, the Lia Fail determined the choice of ancient Irish kings at Tara. Candidates for the throne had to pass a test of sitting upon this mysterious stone, which screamed if he was the legitimate ruler.

The Lia Fail also figures in an Irish story, *Baile in Scáil,* that, Richard Cavendish wrote, "seems to have inspired several features of Perceval's visit to the Grail castle." After discovering the stone in the tale, Conn of the Hundred Battles loses his way in a mist and comes upon a horseman who invites him to a palace that possesses otherworldly qualities. At the palace, Conn is greeted by his host, none other than the god Lugh, who sits on a golden throne alongside a beautiful young woman.

The possible connection between stone and Grail suggested in *Baile in Scáil* is made much more than that in Wolfram von Eschenbach's *Parzival.* There, the Grail *is* a stone.

THE POWER OF THE STONE

Parzival is considered exceptional by most Grail scholars mainly for two reasons. First, because of its literary value – Joseph Campbell, in particular, trumpeted its quality and depth of meaning. Secondly, because in it the Grail takes on a form remarkably unlike the ways it appears elsewhere.

"Its name," Wolfram wrote, "is *lapis exilis.* Campbell notes that this "is one of the terms applied in alchemy to the philosophers stone: 'the uncomely stone, the small or paltry stone'" that would be overlooked by all but the exceptional seeker. "By the power of that stone," Wolfram continues, "the phoenix burns and becomes ashes, but the ashes restore it speedily to life." This phoenix "molts and thereafter very brightly shines." Wolfram goes on to describe how this phoenix-stone affords health and longevity, perhaps even immortality.

But what does this have to do with AM?

If you were to walk into the woods and pass by an *Amanita muscaria* in its initial above-the-ground stage, it would look like one of two things. If rain had not splattered it with mud too much or if the matter of the forest had not settled on it too dustily, it would look like a bright, white little egg. Or, if it had been covered to some extent by brown mud, dirt and other litter, it would look like a common stone - that "uncomely..., small or paltry stone" that Campbell mentions.

And what will happen to this stone some hours after a person has passed by and taken little or no notice of it? It will, like a phoenix, rise and spread its "wings" - signifying the lowly mushroom's capacity for "dying," disappearing and reappearing in full glory. In itself, this would have seemed magical to our ancestors. But add the visionary consequences that followed ingestion of this strange uprising, and you have an alchemy that engenders great stories, legends and myths.

GRAIL IMPLEMENTS IN WOLFRAM'S *PARZIVAL*

Let us linger a bit more with Wolfram's work before we move on.

Jung and Von Franz devote an entire chapter to "The Table, the Carving Platter and the Two Knives." The carving platter is the one already discussed here in Chrétien's story. The table and two knives appear in *Parzival.* They also indicate a connection to the AM ritual.

The Grail Table, Jung and Von Franz believe, was clearly "used for a *meal* [their emphasis]." Carried in immediately after the lance, this table, upon which the Grail will be placed, also has a suggestive appearance. It is, as Jung and Von Franz describe it, "of translucent garnet hyacinth (a reddish stone) with two ivory supports." Again, the pattern of the red crown held up by the white stem. The authors of *The Grail Legend* see in this table not only a relationship to the Round Table of King Arthur's Court but also to the table upon which the fish is set beside the Grail by Brons in Robert de Boron's *Joseph of Arimathea.*

The two knives that are part of the procession in Wolfram, Jung and Von Franz assert, "appear to have the unchanging function of carrying on or completing the work of the lance." As we have seen regarding the bleeding lance in Chrétien, these stand for the implements used in the original ritual to slice the sacred mushroom.

In addition, Jung and Von Franz note a relationship between these tools and how the holy lance in the ritual of the Greek Orthodox Church is employed. It is, they say, "used to cut up the Host on the paten [plate], or the bread is pierced with a lance to indicate the Slaying of the Lamb. According to the liturgy of St. Chrysostom, it was carried in procession with the chalice and the paten."

And, finally, would the lamb itself symbolize, in this case and others, *Amanita muscaria.* Merely look at the fluffy white deposits on the cap of the mushroom for the answer.

AM IN OTHER ELEMENTS OF THE GRAIL LEGEND

THE FOREST

Those in quest of the Grail frequently find themselves winding their way through deep, thick woods. The fertile forest is one of the legend's most dominating and haunting elements for several reasons.

First of all, the forest represents the obstacle through which anyone on a mysterious, dangerous quest must pass to reach the known or unknown goal. Riding into such a dark, foreboding place calls for courage and promises long-hidden treasure.

Paradoxically, however, Jung and von Franz point out, deep woods can offer protection. "With its plant and animal life, its twilight and its restricted horizon, the forest aptly illustrates the as yet barely conscious condition of the child, close to nature as he is. This primitive state is emphasized by the fact that Perceval is fatherless and knows only his mother, who brings him up in loneliness, far from the world.

"Understood as protecting and nourishing nature, the forest also represents the all-embracing quality of the mother..."

The forest is also the place where *Amanita muscaria*, the original Grail, was and is found. This mushroom grows *only* beneath certain trees – including the pine, the oak and the birch – in relationship with their roots.

Finally, a journey into the forest might represent the perils and promise of the psychedelic "trip" – whether that experience is caused by AM or something else. As Richard Cavendish wrote in *King Arthur and the Grail*:

"The forest is an otherworld, a realm which man has not tamed... The forest is the territory of wild nature in both its life-giving and its destructive aspects. Since it is unexplored and dangerous, it has a powerful attraction for the knight errant, whose adventures are set there because there is no straight path through the forest and distractions and entanglements are legion."

Just as the consumption of a hallucinogen such as AM takes the mind back into the stream of the unconscious and the ocean of cosmic consciousness, the forest evokes a sense of the primordial and universal.

Cavendish: "One strand in both the magnetic attraction and the terror of the forest is the feeling of its antiquity. It was there before man came. *It conceals beings and secrets older, wiser and infinitely more powerful than man...* [Italics mine]. In modern psychological terms the uncanny forest represents the dark depths of the mind, the tangled growths of the unconscious, 'old' and 'wild' in the sense of being primitive, instinctive, unmastered by reason. The hero who penetrates the forest is entering a region in himself. This he must do if he is to discover and achieve his complete and true self, but the territory he enters is not only potentially rewarding but highly dangerous. The forest is the place where reason snaps."

And, though Cavendish makes no references to drugs himself, he does make the connection between the experience of the quester for the Grail and the shaman who enters a trance.

Speaking of the hero's entry into the otherworld in the Grail legend and similar myths, he writes: "It seems likely that this pattern goes back ultimately to the practices of the shamans, or priest-magicians, of prehistoric tribes... The shaman's trance-experiences support the modern psychological interpretation of heroic legends, in which the otherworld that the hero invades is his own unconscious mind. It is there, in the darkest and most perilous regions of human nature, where the springs of character and action lie, that he wins his victory and discovers truth."

THE WASTELAND

In the Grail legend the Wasteland results after the key to a land's fertility and to the curing of its people is lost or in danger of being lost. That key is the Grail and/or what it contains, and it represents *Amanita muscaria*.

Why would it have been lost? Because of natural catastrophe, such as a drought, AM may not appear for several years. Or, perhaps due to suppression from outside forces, knowledge of the mushroom's powers might be lost or kept such a closed secret that those powers cannot be widely utilized. Or else, knowledge of *how* to utilize those powers – how to find and prepare and properly administer the healing sacrament – may be lost or kept too much a secret.

In Celtic and other tribes where the knowledge of AM was held only by the presiding druid or shaman, or where it was felt that only a very rare individual could properly apply the powers of the mushroom, a crisis ensued when that shaman grew elderly and/or ill. It became imperative to find a worthy successor. This finding and testing of the candidates for the position is symbolized by the Fisher King/young knight relationship in the Grail legend.

During the time when the old shaman wanes and the new shaman has not yet been initiated and anointed, the land deteriorates into a Wasteland - physically, psychologically and morally.

THE PERILOUS CHAPEL, THE CEMETARY AND THE DEAD BODY

In a chapter of *From Ritual to Romance* called "The Perilous Chapel," Jessie Weston points out that in some Grail romances the hero "meets with a strange and terrifying adventure in a mysterious Chapel, an adventure which, we are given to understand, is fraught with extreme peril to life."

The nature of this ominous place varies from tale to tale. "[S]ometimes there is a Dead Body laid on the altar; sometimes a Black Hand extinguishes the tapers; there are strange and threatening voices, and the general impression is that this is an adventure in which supernatural, and evil, forces are engaged."

Perceval comes across such a chapel in both the Second and Third Continuations to *Le Conte du Graal.* In the second, while seeking the Grail Castle during the night, he believes he sees a huge oak tree upon whose branches are many lighted candles.

However, when he tries to ride toward it, he loses sight of it, but comes upon a little chapel with a single candle burning in its open door. Inside he finds the body of a dead knight, covered with samite. Another candle burns near the corpse's feet.

"Perceval remains some time," Weston notes, "but nothing happens. At midnight he departs; scarcely has he left the Chapel when, to his great surprise, the light is extinguished."

When he reaches the Grail Castle the next day, the Fisher King asks him where he passed the night before. When Perceval tells him of the chapel, the king sighs but says nothing.

In the Third Continuation, the Fisher King is more forthcoming. He tells Perceval the chapel had been built by a queen who was then killed by her own son. Since that time many knights have been killed there, most probably by a mysterious Black Hand which reaches out to extinguish any candle lit there. "The enchantment," Weston says, "can only be put an end to if a valiant knight will fight the Black Hand, and, taking a veil kept in the Chapel, will dip it in holy water, and sprinkle the walls, after which the enchantment will cease."

Much later in the story Perceval - no surprise - becomes that valiant knight. He severely wounds the Black Hand, but when tries to take hold of the veil a "Head" appears. This transforms into the Devil, who seizes Perceval and renders him unconscious. However, upon reviving, Perceval is able to find the veil and sprinkle the walls as instructed.

After sleeping in the chapel overnight, Perceval sees a belfry nearby and rings the bell. An old priest appears and tells him that he has buried three thousand knights slain by the Black Hand in a cemetery created by the queen who had built the chapel. Here, as Weston notes, appears the theme of the chapel-associated Perilous Cemetery. In the Perceval-related Welsh tale *Perlesvaus,* a similar cemetery is surrounded by ghosts of knights who had been slain in the forest and buried in unconsecrated ground.

And even in the earliest-known Grail story, *Le Conte du Graal,* there is a mention of a mystical cemetery. During the section describing Arthur and his knights on the way to the siege of the Chastel Orgueilleux, they meet and eat with some "hermits" who tell them of a certain...

"...graveyard's mysterious spell,

Its wonders so diverse and great

No one alive could now relate

Or even dream that there could be

Such things as these for men to see."

These incidents, plus more that Weston cites from *Perlesvaus* and elsewhere, constitute, she emphasizes in italics, *"the story of an initiation."* In the Middle Eastern mystery religions to which she believes the Grail legend can be ultimately traced, there was a ritual that "comprised a double initiation." The "lower" part of this initiation was an entryway into "the mysteries of generation, i.e., of physical Life; the higher, into the Spiritual Divine Life, where man is made one with God."

And, she concludes, "the tradition of the Perilous Chapel, which survives in the Grail romances in confused and contaminated form, was a reminiscence of the test for this lower initiation."

Indeed, we find exactly this sort of test being part of the typical initiation of a shamanic candidate described in texts on the subject – including Eliade's *Shamanism.* On page 45 of that work the author tells of an explorer investigating Australian aborigines who reported that among the Port Jackson tribes "one became a medicine man if one slept on a grave." More recent studies, Eliade adds, "have fully confirmed and supplemented these accounts." For example: "To make a medicine man, the Euahlayi have the following procedure. They carry the chosen young man to a cemetery and leave him there, bound, for several nights."

Similar practices take place in shamanism's birthplace, Siberia. On page 82, Eliade writes: "The role of the souls of the dead in choosing the future shaman is important in places outside Siberia as well. Eskimo, Australians, and others too, who wish to become medicine men lie by graves; this custom survived even among some historical peoples (e.g., the Celts)."

And, most enlighteningly, Eliade states on page 382 that among Northern European peoples a "prophet becomes such by sitting on tombs, a 'poet' (that is, one inspired) by sleeping on a poet's grave. The same custom is found among the Celts; the *fili* (poet) ate raw bull's flesh, drank the blood, and then slept wrapped in the hide....;

Could the "raw bull" whose flesh and blood were consumed by the *fili* have originally been *Amanita muscaria*, which, we have seen, is (as Soma) symbolized as a bull?

Supporting this conjecture is yet another incident Weston cites in her "The Perilous Chapel" chapter. In the *Queste del saint Graal* "Gawain and Hector de Maris come to an old and mined Chapel where they pass the night. Each has a marvelous dream." In his dream, Gawain dreams of bulls, and the author makes quite a point of the fact that these bulls are all "proud" and "dappled" except for three. And even one of these three bears "traces of spots."

THE FIVE STAGES OF THE GRAIL

Geoffrey Ashe, in his essay "The Grail of the Golden Age" (included in John Matthews' collection *At the Table of the Grail*), notes the curious way the author of *Perlesvaus* "hints at a mystery of transformation, speaking of the Grail as manifesting in five successive ways, finally changing into a chalice. What were its previous guises, how did they lead up to the last? He never says."

These "Five Stages of the Grail," as noted in the previous chapter, have also puzzled several other scholars. Now, at last, with the explanation *of Amanita muscaria* at the origin of the legend, we finally have a solution to that puzzle.

Among the most fascinating things about AM are its stages of growth. These stages, counting only those which can be observed aboveground, can easily be broken down into five:

The "egg" stage. AM first appears as a round, white object – looking like a bird's egg or a golf ball. This is the unbroken volva which contains the hidden cap and stem.

The "breakthrough" stage. Like a hatching chicken, the cap and stem break through the top of the volva. At this point, the cap is rounded and relatively small and clings tightly to the stem.

The "gill-bearing" stage. The part of the cap circling the stem detaches itself, forming its outside edge and bearing the spore-carrying gills underneath the cap.

The "peak" stage. The mushroom grows to its full height. The cap has stretched out to form the classic curved mushroom shape. Surrounding a section of the long white stem more than halfway up is a white "ring," a remnant of the separation of cap and stem, which looks like a torn doll's skirt from the side. The bottom of the stem is bulbous.

The "post-peak" stage. The cap either becomes completely flat, resembling a plate, or curves concavely, with the edge buckling up. This is the "chalice" stage described by the author of *Perlesvaus.*

EPILOGUE: AM AT THE DAWN OF MYTH

If my theory about *Amanita muscaria* and the Holy Grail is true, what are the implications?

It might mean that AM played a part in several other myths and traditions – particularly those that scholars have linked to the Grail legend. Through these we can work our way back to the ur-myth that lies behind them all.

THE TAROT

In the central episode of the earliest-known Grail narrative, Chrétien's *Le Conte du Graal*, Perceval is presented with a sword and then observes a procession that includes a lance, the Grail itself and a carving dish. In Wolfram's *Parzival*, the processional instruments consist of two candlesticks, four candles and a table, four more candles, two silver knives, six glass lights and then the Grail itself (borne by twenty-five women). In other versions, the Grail is often identified as a chalice.

Several scholars (among them Jesse Weston and A.E. Waite) have pointed out the approximate correspondence of these implements to the four suits of the Tarot's "Minor Arcana" (56 of its 78 cards) – swords of Tarot corresponding to sword, of course, cups to chalice, coins/pentacles to carving dish (indeed, the "coins" of the Tarot are closer to the size of dishes than coins), wands/clubs to lance.

The last of these surmises may be incorrect, or at least have an extra meaning. In the oldest complete Tarot deck, the Marseilles, the clubs are clearly rendered as cut tree branches. I believe they refer the Tree of Life at the base of which the Grail (i.e., *Amanita muscaria)* grows.

In *The Grail Seeker's Companion*, John Matthews and Marian Green expand upon these alignments by relating each of the 22 remaining "trumps" (or Major Arcana) to a "suggested" Grail character or element and with a "magical," archetypal image. While some of these are rather far-fetched, others are quite revealing – i.e. the Fool with Perceval, the Magician with Merlin, the Wheel of Fortune with the Round Table, and the Hanged Man with the Fisher King (and with the "magical image" of the Fish).

In his fascinating history *The Occult,* Colin Wilson wrote that he, like many who have contemplated the Tarot, found the images there too puzzling to interpret. However, he insisted, the pack "so obviously *means* something [emphasis his]. Whoever created it or constructed it meant something quite definite by its symbols."

Wilson was particularly intrigued by one of the 22 cards of the Major Arcana, the Hanged Man, which earns a place in Eliot's *The Waste Land* and is considered by many students of the Tarot to be the most intriguing. This card presents a most curious picture: a man hanging from a gibbet by a rope tied to one of his feet. As Wilson says, "The other leg is bent, and its lower part crosses the other leg at right angles, making a *tau* cross. Oddly enough, the face has no expression of suffering, and there is a golden halo around his head..."

Various scholars have connected the Hanged Man with the myths of gods who are killed (usually through hanging or dismemberment) and buried, then attain resurrection. Might not this figure specifically symbolize one or both of two things related to *Amanita muscaria:* the hanging of the AM "god" to dry in the sun, and the initiate who is "turned upside down" by his first psychedelic experience?

Another card that has especially interested students of the Tarot is the only one in the Major Arcana not to be numbered – the Fool. No one has ever been able to explain satisfactorily why the Fool has no number, and frustrated explicators have placed him where they think he belongs – at the beginning, or at the end, or just before the last card, The World.

I assert that the Fool has no number and no particular position because he represents the initiate in the secret ritual. It is he whose stumbling yet steady progress is told symbolically by the cards of the Major Arcana. The Fool is indeed the equivalent of Perceval in the Grail tales. However, there are significant differences.

The Grail legend recounts in coded form the (generally failed) search for one worthy to be the ailing tribal leader's shaman. The tools for the ritual are presented, but the initiation and subsequent rituals never take place.

However, the Tarot represents the initiation itself, where the sacrament is consumed and the novice goes through all the important stages. The Grail story came out of sacred AM use in the northwestern part of Europe; though it's not yet possible to pinpoint the origin of the Tarot illustrations, they relate more to the areas where the "mystery religions" were practiced – particularly southeastern Europe and the Middle East.

Relatively little is known about what went on during the initiatory rites of the Eleusinian Mysteries and similar practices throughout the eastern Mediterranean area, but many modem scholars have accepted the notion that they involved the use of a psychedelic agent. But there is no certainty about which one it might have been.

Nonetheless, in recent years, one theory has been widely accepted – even though it is patently ridiculous.

Oddly enough, when R. Gordon Wasson, who'd written *Soma: Divine Mushroom of Immortality*, came to later co-author a book on the Eleusinian Mysteries (with LSD discoverer Albert Hofmann), he didn't propose AM or any other mushroom as the ritual's secret. Instead, Wasson and Hofmann believed that ergot, the parasitic grain fungus from which Hofmann had synthesized LSD, was the answer.

Why? Because the Eleusinian initiates were sometimes reported to have consumed a barley-based liquid at the start of the rites.

Ergot-infested barley, however, makes little sense for two reasons:

1. If keeping the Mysteries secret was so important (indeed, the word "mystery" originally meant "keeping the mouth shut"), then anything specifically named is almost certainly a red herring or a symbol. If the barley was indeed the source of the sacrament it would hardly be named so clearly.

2. Ergot is *not* a useful psychedelic of itself; in fact, it is an infamously hellish one, causing tormenting sensations, madness and sometimes death. True, LSD can be derived from it, but the ancient Greeks were not capable of such a synthesis.

A much more simple and sensible candidate is a mushroom - if not AM, then another like *Panaeolus papilionaceus*, as Robert Graves suggested.

ALCHEMY

In *A History of Religious Ideas*, Mircea Eliade summed up and revised the work of a lifetime. His three-volume set contains several chapters that tie together various strands of mythology into newly coherent wholes. One of the most brilliant examples is the chapter on

"Hellenistic Alchemy" in Volume Two. There the renowned scholar shows more clearly than anyone had before the connections between early European alchemy and aspects of the Mystery religions.

First of all, and like Jung before him, Eliade rejects the concept that the original role of alchemy was the creation of real or false gold. Gold was merely a symbol of something gold-like to be attained through "the Great Work." Instead, Eliade concludes, alchemy at this stage had more to do with "the discovery of *living* substance [emphasis his]," with "the conception of a complex and dramatic life of matter." And: "We have good reason to suppose that the experience of the dramatic life of matter was made possible by *knowledge of the Greco-Oriental Mysteries"* [emphasis mine].

"The scenario of the 'sufferings,' 'death,' and 'resurrection' of matter is documented in Greco-Egyptian alchemical literature from its beginning," writes Eliade, who next cites the most famous dream of the earliest known alchemical writer, Zosimus. In this vision, "a personage named Ion reveals to him that he was wounded by a sword, cut to pieces, beheaded, flayed, and burned by fire, and that he suffered all this 'in order to be able to change his body into spirit'."

As Eliade writes: "It should be noted not only that Zosimus' description is reminiscent of the dismemberment of Dionysus and the other 'dying gods' of the Mysteries... but that it exhibits striking analogies with the initiatory visions of shamans and, in general, with the fundamental schema of all archaic initiations."

And so, early alchemy, like the Mysteries, may deal with the relatively simple process of the growth, removal, preparation, ingestion, and symbolic "replanting" of AM. But what of the alchemy that crops up in medieval and Renaissance times and resulted in more than 100,000 volumes describing the most complex and baffling procedures? Some of these, too, may have referred to AM.

The most common method of consuming *Amanita muscaria* is fairly simple: dry the mushrooms in the sun or in a 120-160 degree oven and eat from one to three specimens. However, while that approach may work fine with AM that grows in Siberia, it may not work so well elsewhere.

There is considerable evidence that the mushroom's color and chemical makeup varies from region to region. Perhaps this explains the more convoluted methods of preparation one comes across. With certain varieties of AM (which may ultimately be classified separately from the *muscaria*), it might be necessary to take such steps as combining the contents of several specimens to balance the chemicals, to boil these and separate the residue from the remainder, or to take even more involved measures.

AM remains a mystery in itself. There is continuing uncertainty over the chemical components of the fungus among scientists. In fact, up until the 1970s it was mistakenly thought that the main psychedelic agents in AM were muscarine, atropine and bufotenin. More careful laboratory examination showed that there is actually only trace amounts of muscarine in the *muscaria*, and probably no atropine or bufotenin!

Instead, the chief alkaloids are now thought to be muscimole, ibotenic acid and muscazone – but even that may not be correct. Part of the confusion could be due to the region from which the examined specimens were taken; reports on the unpredictable and often unpleasant effects of the North American variety indicate that its chemical composition may differ radically from Asian and European samples. (And this may also explain why there is a known history of AM use by only one Native American tribe).

In any case, several methods of AM preparation have emerged, and others probably exist. Among the reported procedures are: 1) boiling and removing the yellow scum that forms on the liquid's surface which the preparer then "purees further" into a form that is then dried and smoked rather than ingested (in Pynchon's *Gravity's Rainbow*); 2) drying near a fire for a "fortnight [two weeks] or more" and then grinding the result into "a black powder" (from the British underground magazine *Oz* in the early 1970s); and 3) peeling off the cap and soaking it in either brine, vinegar, wine or milk (somewhat similar to the process through which Soma is put in the *Rig-Veda).*

All of these methods are reminiscent of alchemy. The more complex processes of medieval alchemy may have referred to once-discovered, disguised, and eventually lost methods of separating the "essential" chemicals of AM from the unwanted ones, resulting in the potent "Philosopher's Stone."

The relationship between the Grail legend and alchemy is clearest regarding the properties of the Grail and those of this Stone. Traditionally, the Stone, like the Grail, contained the secret to health, abundance, enlightenment and even immortality. It had the greatest spiritual significance, uniting man with God.

As Campbell writes in *Creative Mythology:* "In Wolfram's text the Grail is a stone. 'Its name, he declares, 'is *lapis exilis,'* which is one of the terms applied in alchemy to the philosopher's stone...

"'By the power of that stone,' we read in Wolfram, 'the phoenix burns and becomes ashes, but the ashes restore it speedily to life.' The stone, that is to say, will bring us not only to the *nigredo* and *putrefactio* of the alchemical love-death, but also back to the world – as gold."

THE ORIGINAL MYTH

We can, then, trace alchemy, the Grail legend, Tarot cards and much else back to the vegetation cults of ancient societies. What, then, constituted the ur-myth, the original form of the symbolic story that evolved or degraded into these later forms? I believe we find the nearest thing to it in mythology surrounding Dionysus, that Greek figure who was both god and son of god (Zeus) – and even, in his later representation as Orpheus, son of the son of god!

Twentieth-century science discovered that the human brain is divided between left and right hemispheres that respectively represent the "taking care of business" side and the creative/unbridled side of our nature. Yet long before they knew this, people spoke of the Apollonian and Dionysian halves of behavior.

J.G. Frazer wrote in *The Golden Bough* that Dionysus' "ecstatic worship" was "characterized by wild dances, thrilling music, and tipsy excess." He was "a god of trees," and "particularly sacred to him" was the pine, under which the *Amanita muscaria* is most likely to grow in the Grecian region. Yet Dionysus was not symbolic of a tree. "[H]is rude effigy is depicted appearing out of a low tree or bush, and images of this god were phallic and had 'red faces'." He is likened to a bull, and some people found in this tradition" the clue to the bovine shape in his being "reported to have been the first to yoke oxen to the plough" (think of how AM "plows" up from the earth and of the Soma/bull comparisons).

In the mysteries, Dionysus is presented as a phallus cradled in a winnowing basket, just as AM is "cradled" in the basket-like volva from which it is born. Dionysus "died a violent death," his ambushers "rushed upon him, cut him limb from limb, boiled his body with various herbs, and ate it. But his sister Minerva, who had shared in the deed, kept his heart and gave it to [Zeus]," through whose power his son was "brought to life again."

If Dionysus is substituted for Persephone in the Eleusinian Mysteries, we can come even closer to determining the ur-myth. Is it fair to do so? Not only fair, but it solves many incongruous aspects of this myth.

As Frazer notes of Demeter and Persephone: "Substantially their myth is identical with the Syrian one of Aphrodite (Astarte) and Adonis, the Phrygian one of Cybele and Attis, and the Egyptian one of Isis and Osiris. In the Greek fable, as in its Asiatic and Egyptian counterparts, a goddess mourns the loss of a loved one, who personifies the vegetation... which dies in winter to revive in spring; only whereas the Oriental imagination figured the loved and lost one as a dead lover or a dead husband lamented by his lamenter, his wife, Greek fancy embodied the same idea in the... form of a dead daughter bewailed by her sorrowing mother."

One other curious thing that Frazer and many others have remarked on is the similarity between Demeter and Persephone. They are so alike as to seem aspects of the same person. One more point to keep in mind: Though Dionysus is the son of Zeus and Symele in some versions of his birth, he is the son of Zeus and either Demeter or Persephone in others.

It is possible now to understand what most likely happened: The inventive Greeks not only took existing myths about the dying and resurrecting vegetation god and transformed them into Dionysus/Bacchus/Orpheus, but also added their own variations – most notably the compelling myth of the abduction of one vegetation deity by the god of the underworld, and the mother of the abducted one (herself also a vegetation deity) reacting by bringing about a waste land on earth until her offspring is returned.

Only it would not do to have a male figure, Dionysus, be the abductee, so Persephone was invented (though given little character of her own separate from Demeter's) to play the part.

The ur-myth behind these and subsequent traditions, then, may have been something like this:

When all was well, when people paid proper homage to the gods and goddesses of Nature – chiefly through sacrificing part of each (seed or spore-containing) crop to the earth goddess – the deprivations of the winter wasteland are followed in the spring by the magical gifts of the deities. The sun returns, the rain and lightning come, and humanity's sustenance grows from the earth.

First to appear, merely hours after the rains, are the spring mushrooms, sons and daughters of the Sky Father and the Earth Mother. Eventually they are joined by the one that is the most dazzling, both in terms of its appearance and its holy revelations when eaten.

Since the eating of a god is a particularly awesome and perilous action, a ritual ensuring the god's resurrection must accompany the act. Participants must be initiated into the proper way to carry out the ritual. Soon after the enactment of this ritual the first flowers and crops begin to appear – and the cycle of life is assured once more.

Bibliography

WORKS CITED

Allegro, John M. *The Sacred Mushroom and the Cross*. New York, Doubleday, 1970.

Ashe, Geoffrey. "The Grail of the Golden Age." From *At the Table of the Grail*. John Matthews, ed. London, Watkins, 2004.

________. *King Arthur's Avalon: The Story of Glastonbury*. New York, Barnes and Noble, 1997.

Campbell, Joseph. *The Masks of God: Creative Mythology*. New York, Penguin, 1991.

Cavendish, Richard. *King Arthur and the Grail: The Arthurian Legends and Their Meaning*. New York, Taplinger, 1979.

Cavendish, Richard, Amanda Harman & Brian Innes, eds. *Man, Myth and Magic: The Illustrated Encyclopedia of Mythology, Religion and the Unknown*. Singapore, Marshall Cavendish, 1995 (revised edition).

Chayefsky, Paddy. *Altered States*. Bantam, 1981.

Comfort, W. W., trans. *The Quest of the Holy Grail*. Cambridge, Ontario, In Parentheses Publications, Old French Series, 2000. Translation of *La Queste del Saint Graal*. Albert Pauphilet , ed. Paris, Librairie Ancienne Honoré Champion, 1921.

Cowan, Tom. *Fire in the Head: Shamanism and the Celtic Spirit*. New York, Harper One , 1993

Cunliffe, Barry. *The Ancient Celts*. New York, Penguin, 1999.

De Boron, Robert. "Joseph D'Arimathe" and "Merlin." From *Romanz De L'estoire Dou Graal*. W.A. Nitze, ed. Paris, Librairie Ancienne Honoré Champion, 1971.

De Troyes, Chrétien. *Le Conte del Graal (Parsifal)*. From *Arthurian Romances*. D.D.R. Owen, trans. London, J.M. Dent, 1987.

Dillon, Miles, ed. & trans. "*Baile in Scáil*: the Phantom's Frenzy." From *The Cycle of the Kings*. Oxford University Press, 1946.

Eliade, Mircea. *A History of Religious Ideas. Volume One: From the Stone Age to the Eleusinian Mysteries*. Willard R. Trask, trans. University of Chicago Press, 1978.

________. *Shamanism: Archaic Techniques of Ecstasy*. New York, Princeton/ Bollingen, 1964.

Eliot, T.S. *The Waste Land*. London, Horace Liveright, 1922.

Encyclopedia Britannica. Eleventh edition. Cambridge University Press, 1911.

Eschenbach, von, Wolfram. *Parzival*. London, Penguin, 1980.

Evans, Sebastian, trans. *Perlesvaus (The High History of the Holy Grail)*. Cambridge, James Clarke, 1969.

Frazer, James G. *The Golden Bough*. New York, Macmillan, 1922.

Furst, Peter T. *Hallucinogens and Culture*. Novato, Calif., Chandler and Sharp, 1976.

Geoffrey of Monmouth. *The Life of Merlin, Vita Merlini*. John Jay Parry, trans. Hong Kong, Forgotten Books, 2008.

Graves, Robert. *The White Goddess: A Historical Grammar of Poetic Myth*. London, Faber and Faber, 1966.

________. "Mushrooms and Religion" and "The Two Births of Dionysus." From *Difficult Questions, Easy Answers*. New York, Doubleday, 1973.

________. *Food for Centaurs: Stories, talks, critical studies, poems*. New York, Doubleday, 1960.

________. "Centaur's Food." *Atlantic Monthly*, August 1956.

________. Review of Wasson's *Soma*. *Atlantic Monthly*, August 1957.

Harner, Michael J. *Way of the Shaman*. New York, Harper and Row, 1980.

Jochelson, Waldemar. *The Koryak* (Vol. 6 of Publications, Jesup North Pacific Expedition). New York, AMS Press, 1908.

Jung, Carl. *Aion: Researches into the Phenomenology of the Self*. Gerhard Adler, trans. New York, Bollingen, 1959.

________. *Memories, Dreams, Reflections*. New York, Random House, 1963.

Jung, Emma and von Franz, Marie-Louise. *The Grail Legend*. Princeton, N.J., Princeton University Press, 1998.

La Barre, Weston. "My Friend Gordon." From *The Sacred Mushroom Seeker: Essays for R. Gordon Wasson*. Thomas J. Riedlinger, ed. Rochester, Vermont. Park Street Press, 1990.

________. Review of Wasson's *Soma*. *American Anthropologist*, April, 1970.

Lacy, Norris J, ed. *The Arthurian Encyclopedia*. New York, Peter Bedrick Books, 1986.

Langsdorf, von, G. H. *Divine Mushroom of Immortality (Fly Agaric Kamachadal)*. Frankfurt 1809. Complete (unattributed) translation reprinted in Canadian Whole Earth Almanac, Vol. 3 no. 1, 1972.

Levi-Strauss, Claude. Review of Wasson's *Soma* in *L'Homme*, cited on dust jacket.

Loomis, Roger Sherman. *The Grail: From Celtic Myth to Christian Symbol*. Princeton, N.J., Princeton University Press, 1991.

________. *Celtic Myth and Arthurian Romance*. Chicago, Academy Chicago Publishers, 2005.

Malory, Thomas. *Le Morte D'Arthur*. Stephen H. A. Shepherd, ed. New York, Norton, 2003. First published by William Caxton, 1485.

Markale, Jean. *Merlin: Priest of Nature*. Rochester, Vermont, Inner Traditions, 1995.

________. *The Celts: Uncovering the Mythic and Historic Origins of Western Culture.* Rochester, Vermont, Inner Traditions, 1993.

________. *The Grail: The Celtic Origins of the Sacred Icon*. Rochester, Vermont, Inner Traditions, 1982.

Matthews, John and Marian Green. *The Grail Seeker's Companion: A Guide to the Grail Quest in the Aquarian Age*. London, Thorsons, 1986

Matthews, John, ed. *At the Table of the Grail*. London, Routledge and Kegan Paul, 1984.

Nutt, Alfred. *Studies on the Legend of the Holy Grail*. London, David Nutt, 1888.

O'Flaherty, Wendy Doniger, trans. *Rig-Veda*. New York, Penguin, 1981.

Puharich, Andrija. *The Sacred Mushroom: Key to the Door of Eternity.* New York, Doubleday, 1959.

Pynchon, Thomas. *Gravity's Rainbow*. New York, Penguin, 1995.

Riedlinger, Thomas J., editor. *The Sacred Mushroom Seeker: Tributes to R. Gordon Wasson*. Rochester, Vermont. Park Street Press, 1990.

Roach, William, ed. *The Didot Perceval.* Philadelphia, University of Pennsylvania Press, 1941.

Robbins, Tom. "Superfly: The Toadstool That Conquered the Universe." *High Times,* December, 1976.

Ross, Anne. "The Celts." From *Man, Myth and Magic*.

Rudgley, Richard. *The Alchemy of Culture: Intoxicants in Society.* London, British Museum Press, 1993)

________. *The Encyclopedia of Psychoactive Substances.* New York, St. Martin's Press, 1998.

Schroeder, von, Leopold. *Mysterium und Mimus im Rig-Veda*. Leipzig, H. Haessel, 1908. Available online at archive.org.

Seymour-Smith, Martin. *Robert Graves: His Life and Works*. London, Bloomsbury, 1995.

Siegel, Ronald K. *Intoxication*. Rochester, Vermont, Inner Traditions, 2005.

Skeels, D. trans. *Didot-Perceval (The Romance of Perceval in Prose).* Seattle, University of Washington Press, 1961.

Smith, Huston. "Historical Evidence: India's Sacred Soma." From *Cleansing the Doors of Perception*. New York, Tarcher/Putnam, 2000.

Stevens, Jay. *Storming Heaven: LSD and the American Dream*. New York, Grove/Atlantic, 1987.

Tolstoy, Nikola. *The Quest for Merlin*. New York, Little, Brown, 1985.

Vitebsky, Piers. *The Shaman*. New York, Little, Brown, 1995.

Walker, Barbara. *The Woman's Encyclopedia of Myths and Secrets*. New York, Harper/Collins, 1983.

Wasson, R. Gordon. "Great Adventures III: The Discovery of Mushrooms That Cause Strange Visions." *Life* magazine, May 13, 1957.

_________. *Soma: Divine Mushroom of Immortality*. London, Harcourt/Brace, 1968.

Weil, Andrew T. *The Natural Mind: A New Way of Looking at Drugs and the Higher Consciousness*. Boston, Houghton Mifflin, 1972.

_________. Article. *The Journal of Psychoactive Drugs*, Oct.-Dec., 1988.

_________. Article, *High Times*, May 1982.

Weston, Jessie L. *From Ritual to Romance*. New York, Doubleday Anchor Books, 1957.

Wilson, Colin. *The Occult*. London, Watkins, 2004.

Witchard Goetinck, Glenys. *Peredur: Study of Welsh Tradition in the Grail Legends*. Cardiff, University of Wales Press, 1975

Zimmer, Heinrich. *The King and the Corpse: Tales of the Soul's Conquest of Evil*. Joseph Campbell, ed. Princeton, N.J., Princeton University Press, 1971.

FURTHER READING

Ball, Martin W. *The Entheogenic Evolution: Psychedelics, Consciousness and Awakening the Human Spirit*. Ashland, Ore., Kyandara Publishing, *2008*.

Devereux, Paul. *The Long Trip: A Prehistory of Psychedelia*. Brisbane, Daily Grail Publications, 2008.

Forte, Robert, ed. *Entheogens and the Future of Religion*. Rochester, Vermont, Park Street Press, 2012.

Letcher, Andy. *Shroom: A Cultural History of the Magic Mushroom*. London, Faber & Faber, 2006.

McKenna, Terence. *Food of the Gods: The Search for the Original Tree of Knowledge; A Radical History of Plants, Drugs, and Human Evolution*. New York, Bantam, 1993.

_________. *The Archaic Revival: Speculations on Psychedelic Mushrooms, the Amazon, Virtual Reality, UFOs, Evolution, Shamanism, the Rebirth of the Goddess, and the End of History*. New York, HarperCollins, 1992.

Monaco, Richard. *Parsival or a Knight's Tale*. e-reads.com, 2004.

Powys, John Cowper. *A Glastonbury Romance*. New York, The Overlook Press, 1996.

Ruck, Carl A.P., Mark A. Hoffman and Jose Alfredo Gonzáles Celdrán. *Mushrooms, Myth and Mithras*. San Francisco, City Lights Books, 2011.

Rush, John ed. *Entheogens and the Development of Culture: The Anthropology and Neurobiology of Ecstatic Experience.* Berkeley, North Atlantic Books, 2013.

Tennyson, Alfred. *Idylls of the King.* J.M. Gray, ed. London, Penguin Books, 1983.

White, T.H. *The Once and Future King.* New York, Ace, 1987.

www.ingramcontent.com/pod-product-compliance
Lightning Source LLC
Chambersburg PA
CBHW070753290326
41931CB00011BA/1993

* 9 7 8 0 9 8 8 4 1 2 2 4 8 *